Decomposing Holy Ground

Decomposing Holy Ground

Theological Compost for Shifting Worlds

Emma Lietz Bilecky

scm press

© Emma Lietz Bilecky 2025

Published in 2025 by SCM Press

Editorial office
3rd Floor, Invicta House,
110 Golden Lane,
London EC1Y 0TG, UK
www.scmpress.co.uk

SCM Press is an imprint of Hymns Ancient & Modern Ltd
(a registered charity)

Hymns Ancient & Modern® is a registered trademark of
Hymns Ancient & Modern Ltd
13A Hellesdon Park Road, Norwich,
Norfolk NR6 5DR, UK

All rights reserved. No part of this publication may be reproduced,
stored in a retrieval system, or transmitted,
in any form or by any means, electronic, mechanical,
photocopying or otherwise, without the prior permission of
the publisher, SCM Press.

The Author has asserted her right under the Copyright, Designs and
Patents Act 1988 to be identified as the Author of this Work

British Library Cataloguing in Publication data
A catalogue record for this book is available
from the British Library

978-0-334-06170-0

EU GPSR Authorised Representative
LOGOS EUROPE, 9 rue Nicolas Poussin, 17000, LA ROCHELLE, France
E-mail: Contact@logoseurope.eu

No part of this book may be used or reproduced in any manner for the
purpose of training artificial intelligence technologies or systems.

Typeset by Regent Typesetting

Contents

Preface ix
Introduction xiii

1 Triangulating 1
   Winter solstice 1
   Soil work 2
   Disorientation (a history) 3
   Learning to listen 5
   Troubling landscapes 8
   Decomposition 12
   Grounding: a prayer 16

2 Making *terra nullius* 19
   Spring equinox 19
   Making soil 20
   Terraformation 21
   Prayer plows 23
   Terra nullius and the Doctrine of Discovery 26
   Naming land, claiming land 28
   Land as property 29
   Land as resource 31
   Land as verb 35
   The work of water: a prayer 38

3 Compost Cosmologies   43
   Summer solstice   43
   Everything is compost   43
   Land work   48
   Being compost   50
   Death is not a metaphor   54
   Disintegration, decomposition: a prayer   57

4 The Geography of Sin   59
   Midsummer   59
   Bad faith   61
   Humans in the carbon cycle   63
   Climate hedonism   66
   Structural violence, collective sin   68
   The fire, inferno   72
   After the fire   74
   Climate apocalypse in the built environment   75
   Ongoing: a prayer   76

5 Becoming Place, Fermenting Culture   79
   Fall equinox   79
   Practice makes process   80
   Preserving culture   82
   Space and time   88
   The weight of the world   90
   Transformation: a prayer   94

6 God is Change: Beyond Creation Care   97
   Persephone   97
   Feedback loops   98
   Transforming climate anxiety   101
   Towards experience   104
   From creation care, towards caring, creating 107
   God is a gardener   110
   Seeds: a prayer   111

Preface

The seeds of this book germinated during a fellowship at Princeton Theological Seminary's farm. They called it the 'Farminary', and my job was to think about compost, write about compost and make compost.

Compost was the heart of the Farminary, an experimental, off-campus haven for weary seminarians craving time in their bodies and on the land, away from the classroom. But the ideas of the classroom inevitably crept in, and soon sermons from the compost pile emerged.

I was drawn to this place for its unlikely ability to combine two things I cared very much about: regenerative agriculture and theology. The questions I brought to the farm were theological questions of a sort, but they also reflected the theological context in which I was raised – along with its theological problems. As a still-beginning farmer, I wanted to know what it was that made farmers so consistently the most theological people I'd known, and what it was about the land and land-based work that made it a much better teacher than any priest or pastor at any of the churches I'd spent my life attending. What was happening *here* seemed like what they were talking about *there*, but real. On the farm, resurrection is not a story, but a reality. On the farm, humans collaborate with natural processes to build soil faster than nature would otherwise allow. This seemed more like the work of the people than any liturgy.

At the same time, I wanted to know why it was that agricultural work has been so diminished and derided, and why this work that most people understand to be so simple was so hard in my experience. Why did most people not only lack respect for the work and those who shepherded it but have a such a grave misunderstanding of the work's utter difficulty? Maybe the fact of its difficulty had something to do with its necessity. Maybe the farm was teaching me what my ego and acculturation had been refusing to let me learn.

In learning how to farm, there were so many, countless, difficult lessons I learned through humiliation – things a seasoned farmer would know, but a beginning farmer must fail at in order to learn. Simple lessons: like how much a person at the end of their rope can reasonably accomplish in a day; or that anything that can go wrong, will; or that living plants and animals have needs and desires of their own, and they don't stop living once I stop watching. Wear long sleeves, even in summer. Plan for failure. Check the weather.

What learning to farm revealed in me was deeply disturbing: that I didn't actually believe the earth was alive. I had been raised to treat the living world as a machine, with predictable outputs based on fixed inputs, a machine that could be better understood through calculation than observation. I earnestly expected to be able to control my environment because I conceived of that environment as a lifeless assortment of things from which my life derived lifeless resources. I didn't really believe that the lives constituting that environment were meaningfully like mine.

But, like me, foxes get hungry and sometimes eat chickens. Like me, chickens have a heartbeat that stops without oxygen. Like me, plants experience phases of faster and slower growth and go dormant in winter when there's less energy to go around and more to conserve. Not until learning to farm did my bones know I was part of a living earth – that my being was continuous with that of the soil. Farming showed me this deeply: that the exact minerals and nutrients my body needs to function are those sourced from the erosion of bedrock, through the excrement of insects and the tissues of plants. That the compounds in tomatoes reverse my depletions in the work of tending them in the sun and heat. That the farmers in my family tree gave me these hands especially suited to this work. That everything we touch – not just the food we eat – has its origin in the soil. That eating is one manifestation of our inextricable connection to it.

PREFACE

These lessons are humbling for their simplicity. Lessons we should all learn, and perhaps do, as children. What made these lessons so profound revealed to me the extent to which I had forgotten them. And why? Something to do with what we call religion, I suppose. Religion, not in its ultimate and beautiful purpose to reunite and weave together, but as people traumatized and marginalized by the abuse of religious power know it: as a too-narrow, life-denying fixation on some elsewhere afterlife that prioritizes spiritual purity over the messy care and reciprocity we need for making new worlds. Could it be that the religion of my upbringing was not just responsible for this earthly alienation in me, but had something do with the moment of ecocide in which we find ourselves collectively?

At the Farminary, I found it wasn't easy to merely add 'green' lessons to existing curricula, because the problems we sought to confront were structural. The way through these problems required not cosmetic alterations but entirely new ways of being. This was the impulse of that farm – that becoming different kinds of beings and practising a different kind of religion requires changing the environments that shape our thoughts and actions in the first place. Without environmental change, deep change is nearly impossible.

Learning to farm as a practice of shaping the environment that fed me and so many others began a process of undoing. This book is an attempt to continue that process of undoing by attending to the ground from which we speak, think and imagine our precarious future. This task is no less than religious. Though I am not a very good theologian, I am thinking with soil in religious terms, in the hope that doing so can reconnect and rework real environments that have been harmed by the religious language of sin, separation and damnation that has caused too many to reject our only home.

I want to practise religion as people who know the land do. I want to confront the religion of whiteness that unleashes such harm on land and people by pretending the two are separate. I want to reclaim a religion like that of the farmers, and see what farmers – who already know and navigate climate chaos – can show us about navigating the climate we're creating. I wanted to ask how farmers and farming are contributing to this mounting devastation, and how farmers and farming could contribute to its repair. I do not seek to provide answers, but to find a way through the sticky, intractable problems, going to the places it hurts. This is the kind of prayer I can do.

Introduction

This work is a meditation on lessons learned from soil, a ground that is evolving, never stable.[1] Attention to soil – its time,[2] its scale and its slow pace of change – is more unlearning than achievement. This unlearning mimics the many un-doings always ongoing in healthy, living soil. Another word for this is decomposition. Soil's decomposing movements are not soil's end. Digestion does not make this matter disappear, but simply reworks it, over time transmigrating and fixing that death and decay into the soil profiles that everywhere constitute land, that make the soft ground we stand upon. Death and dying are inherent to the processes of land and placemaking. Still, we must be careful to ask after the conditions that make deaths possible or impossible, necessary or unnecessary, just or unjust, so as not to ordain, reproduce or dismiss inherited violences. There are many violences to which this land is witness.

It is okay not to know. It is better not to presume to know where we are or where we must be headed when still so much is undetermined. Better simply to sit with the facts of *this matter*, our planetary condition, witnessing the enormity of loss accomplished and anticipated, whole worlds passing away as new worlds emerge on a cloudy horizon. Where we are, it is right to be unsure, to suspend judgement long enough to try to make out, even if partially, what is going on. To be *here* and *now* can be hopeful, more hopeful at least than the already-redemptive ending. The tragic ending is too close, it seems, while the redemptive one is too far off, out of reach and out of touch. We stand somewhere in the middle, not seeking evasive assurance that would excuse our action today. We stand on shifting and ephemeral ground as wind carries, floodwaters inundate and charred forests release soil in mudslides. There is no more stability. And we must begin the work where we are.

Our places are, everywhere, replete with death redeemed for profit but not redemptive. As connective threads weave this terrain together, we find suffering shared across space and time. Our living derives from the death of others; our ignorance relies on the suffering of others. Shallow platitudes and hollow assurances do little to assuage the guilt we feel, weak attempts as they are to avoid grief and work both. Grief, instead, deserves to be held tenderly – is asking us, together, to hold it – even as we are held by this shifting ground. No need to hold it together, though. The burden is too big to bear alone in that way.

In an era when climate change is impressing itself upon us, climate forcings *forcing* us to think differently about nearly everything, our once-stable theories and self-concepts reveal themselves fragile. Now we are grasping at new – and older – sites for theological practice, needing new ways to know God that can hold up through such a time as this.[3] We need words – more, we need *practices* – durable for the tasks before us: for rebuilding the environments we inhabit in ways that generate life more than death from now on.

So many of us live in deadly environments these days. As soils hold contaminants, they testify to our addiction to extractives even as forms of extraction change over time. So many of us are shaped by these soils. Legacy leads live on in blood and streams. Children taste dirt instinctively. All the same, city parcels sink life savings, as so-called laws of scarcity and competition govern property relations even where scarce land is poisoned. We are shaped by these environments, despite their complication and construction. But we might yet reject belief in these built environments; in this we have a choice. As we daily participate in their reconstruction, we might still choose ways that foster, rather than inhibit, the living of neighbours seen and unseen, human and more-than-human. Incomprehensible suffering and pervasive pollution are the primary products of so many of the built environments in this tense present,[4] but these environments, perpetually reworked and upheld by engineers, farmers, worms, fungi and everyday theologians, can be reworked again – built now towards something like flourishing. The closest thing to any kind of universal truth I know is this: the ground is *always* being remade by the living and the dead in cooperation. Their traces are written in the soil.

They say we are approaching apocalypse. Others have survived apocalypses already.[5] Apocalypse is less a destiny than an unveiling, making known what is already here. We wait as it comes into focus, looking for clues in cracks that form along fault lines, in the doubts and fears of the would-be faithful. These cracks emergent inside rigid belief systems let light and oxygen in, just as digging forks in compacted beds reinvigorate dormant soil life by making way for life-giving water and air. This is a kind of recomposition through decomposition: in this compost pile, we must all undergo transformation to keep alive and awake as we remake the ruins of Western civilizations. We must change in order to survive. To survive, we must change together.

The compost we make, if we are careful and attentive, is *hot*.[6] The oxygen that our muscles and our digging forks, turning, infuse into the heap feeds innumerable eubacteria – our microscopic collaborators – first. They go on to feed the macroscopic churners – like the lowly earthworm – whose movements and excrements stitch this substance consisting of so much difference together. Fungal webs bridge difference, reaching far and wide to facilitate the sharing of food and nutrients throughout the soil food web. And it is this lively and biodiverse web of life that feeds us, too. Compost is a place of death and life *at the same time*. In here, they are inseparable. This is a place of resignation and hope, where the borders between my life and yours dissolve to make both our lives – and more – possible. Letting go of the quest for individual, internal coherence or immortality, compost collaborators undergo rot together, feeding on the shared immortal body they together create, making new kinds of life possible in civilization's refuse, *ad infinitum*.

Yet, for those of us raised with strict bifurcations between the new and the landfill, opposite poles on a continuum from new life towards death – from economic boom to bust, from profit's possibility to the pollution it produces, from strip mine to earthen reinterment in *not mine*, but my neighbour's backyard, downstream or downwind – we must learn to recognize the recurrent resurrection of all life cycles, including ours. Our lives begin and end in the soil as, daily, our eating recalls.

Over time, the practice of agriculture – from which I had been cut off through multigenerational accidents and achievements that wrested my ancestors from the farms that raised them – has begun to transform me. One day, the eucharistic prayer I had long committed to memory – 'take, eat, this is my body, given for you' – took on fresh meaning abruptly. Now, understanding the cycle folded so seamlessly into countless cultures so as to become almost invisible, suddenly *mattered*. I understood this phrase, not as some abstract metaphor, but as a living process I could taste and see. I could locate this prayer's mattering, now, in the seasonal cycles I witnessed and in which I participated: those that transfigured grass to grain through solar energy, soil's fertility and water's life, undergoing many chromatic and textural transformations before and after harvest. How the bread of life, then, was an entity that folded many lives and living water into its own substance – the hand of the farmer, scattering seed; the hand of the baker, capturing and imparting wild yeast from kneading hands and the thin air we breathe, making this bread rise, making this bread capable of feeding thousands. To say 'this is my body', while holding this bread, is to confess commonality across the cycles that always connect human and humus and effect their mutual remaking, to reverence this holy miracle of ceaseless continuation, and to consecrate that matter which feeds body and soil and soul at once.

Still, I was raised with a deep suspicion of the material world. The religion of my youth served to shelter me from the vulnerability to and care for this earth that are, I now believe, our greatest gift and calling. To be somehow 'in the world, but not of the world' is the cruellest fiction. To be in the world *and of* the world is more honest – a reckoning and a calling for these important times. For the more we internalize the losses and possibilities of this world's ending, the more we see our fate not as divergent from, but as sutured to, the fate of an earth we can love.

A theology hopelessly fixated on individualism reduces our shared existential threats to aggregated individual avarice, or, alternatively, hopes that individual behaviour change will save the world. These conceptions of sin and salvation will not work much longer. For that proposed end of salvation – that is, life – only happens in relation, by definition. Whatever sin is in this so-called Anthropocene comes down to spatial arrangements that guide actions and induce demand more than individual moral failings. The impacted and terraformed environments in and through which we live cause us to harm even that which we love: *I do not do what I want; what I do, I do not want.*

A theology that is not critical of the dynamic, mutually formative processes through which people shape landscapes and landscapes shape people thinks that 'creation care' is merely a matter of changing the lightbulbs. It assumes we know already *how* to care, when this is, in fact, the work we have to do in a place so thoroughly shaped by the violence of Christian colonization. It is this perverted religious impulse that worked to undermine the very possibility of creation's care in the first place, systematically seeking to sever the ties that co-constitute and sustain land and spiritual praxis, together. Care, then, is not merely a verb but mainly a practice; not a belief but an action that can help but also harm. It is a muscle that must be exercised, a capacity to grow. The dictates of alienation and specialization that make us believe time is preciously scarce cause us to shrink from the acts of care that give our lives any substance at all. Part of surviving a changed world is asking: for what and for whom do we hope to survive? For what and for whom do I care?

Many marketable versions of sustainability are impotent to sustain us. Though environmental behaviour change is urgently important, it is only the floor. The gift is in the invitation, not merely to consume less or to eat mindfully, but also, and more fundamentally, to adopt different ways of moving and thinking, praying and believing, transforming our actions and the environments they create. Likewise, at its best the use and power of religious language is not simply to convert minds but to do better theology, theology that is responsive to the existential threats and crises of legitimacy that berate it from every side (for good reason).[7] Crises of legitimacy invite us to re-examine the inherited doctrines we profess or deny, and to instead practise the Resurrection we profess.[8]

The existential threats we live with and anticipate demand changes in patterns of existence, and revisions to future expectations, life plans or salvation narratives. This terrifies many of us (again, for good reason). Our fear lurks under the surface, implicitly informing these decades of denialism and distraction advanced by those who have chosen not to believe or otherwise heed the warnings of scientists and instead occupy another reality on life support. These survival strategies, though deepening rather than avoiding the problem of climate breakdown, yet testify to its magnitude, perhaps even better than those optimists who advocate a way forward requiring only incremental change – substitutions in consumer choices in place of revised patterns of life. In between the lines of polarized scripts, the fear we witness is profound. For this climate change demands radical change, and not only to the way we produce and consume energy, but also to the very words we use to describe our places and our gods. For the words we use reflect and shape our places and our gods together, and our places are changing already.

Through land work, I am returning to older knowledges. Regardless of our ability to value embodied wisdoms, our lives testify to the arts of cultivation, food production and preservation passed on by all the generations who have gone before. Returning to them, I join many others, young and old, who share my concerns about ecological alienation. A new generation of farmers-by-choice, we are committing our lives to caring for the soils we did not see or know before. These embodied wisdoms, nearly lost after being rendered irrelevant to the modern world, are recoverable only by practice. What we practise shapes our beliefs about the world, more than belief directs practice.

Our words about God (which some call theologies) inevitably reflect our places and our practices. They will not be the same everywhere. For too long, Christianity, allied with the powers of imperialism and mission, and armed with the Doctrine of Discovery, has sought a universalizing view, superseding the land's testimony with words from elsewhere that do not touch this ground here. At the same time, this language of redemption refuses to acknowledge the ways it extracts from and is shaped by the ground it does touch. Translating an ancient religion born of Levantine hills and deserts into a religion everywhere the same and contained in a book, modern versions of this religion have developed some bad habits. In some Protestant traditions, they say scripture, tradition, reason and experience help us know the divine. What we often fail to recognize, as a colonial consequence, is how each of these is formed and informed by the colonized places from which they come. Just as dehistoricizing the living text of tradition makes us miss much, decontextualizing our own ways of knowing, and failing to admit the ways our sensing derives from the places we've sensed, can make us miss the wonderfully patchy and partial nature of all religious experience. When we presume access to omniscience, through the tunnel vision of *sola scriptura*, we might neglect to faithfully consult the other living texts that show us ongoing creation in the places we inhabit.

The words of any Christian confession change as worlds change. The land and its Indigenous defenders are getting louder in an age of climate chaos, and the long-delayed impacts of that original rupture confront and challenge once-stable theological truths. Do our planting and harvesting liturgies work the same way in eras of reduced or irregular seasonality? How does the everlasting covenant's emphasis change when the plastic cup with which we remember will persist in our environment *from everlasting to everlasting, the same*? Is God's promise never again to flood the earth still trustworthy, given what our climate models and swelling water cycles predict? Do our words about God stay the same in a changing landscape, or do they need to change, too?

I write through belief, suspended in the middle of these questions, mostly unresolved. They are questions about how taken-for-granted concepts, ways of living and religion (in truth, the same) adapt to a world shifting on sinking sand. A world that is already passing away. I am searching for words about God, now, to do different kinds of work.

Every day, we make choices that reflect our assumptions about the future. We make plans based on a past that seem surer and more stable than the science foretells. We steel ourselves against uncertainty, hoping the unravelling will not be as totalizing or as impactful as we fear. How does one prepare for a future so uncertain? What kinds of risk do we take? The common sense underlying modern economics is misaligned with a planet that cannot sustain the 'normal' we seek in the status quo of endless growth. We know already that the future will be unlike the past, that the lag time between harm and impact at the scale of earth systems means we must learn to live with instability this next century precipitated by the heedlessness of the last one. How do we make decisions, based on today's empirical evidence and yesterday's experience, when many of the assumptions we have come to hold dear will not be able to hold us any longer in the future that is being created for us?

If these questions make you afraid, you are not alone. I wonder if we can sit with that fear together long enough to honour what it sees, resisting the urge to dismiss it simply because it requires something extraordinary of us. A future that is cloudy and uncertain may induce fear, but the ruptures we perceive may offer to us the grounds of renewal and regeneration, if we can *tend* to this ground – *attend* to this circumstance we find ourselves in – keep paying *attention*. Tending shares root with continuation, sustaining. To tend is to expect, to stretch towards, to give heed and to wait.

The patience and persistence of soil invite us to find a way forward even as so many options are daily foreclosed. Soil is a microcosm, a universe of relation unto itself. In every place, soil, as the kind of thing that goes on, resists our simplifications and continues despite despair. Soil is a verb. Soil is us. Soil is God incarnate.[9] We are humans of humus, bound by and to the land separated from the waters, and so many of our origin stories touch the soil. Anishinaabe and Haudenosaunee creation stories tell of Turtle Island's emergence in a muskrat's soil-offering spread on a turtle's back. Hebraic worlds were created from the separation of lands and waters, and then destroyed by the dissolution of this distinction in deluge. Eden is animated by God's exhalation through garden soil, which formed our muddy ancestors. The green growth that the peace-bearing dove picked with its beak from past a drowning sea promised post-apocalyptic survival, a reunion with the soil we will always need.

The loss of soil, then, should register as an existential threat. The loss of soil is a loss of bearing, unsettling origin stories and gods. Colonial violence and its accompanying displacements are a kind of soil loss: wherein political, economic and eugenicist imperatives forcibly separate people from place to enable colonial expansion and fuel capitalist extraction. As a result, many have experienced climate apocalypse already – living in environments beyond recognizability to ancestors who provided the durable instructions for living in places from which descendants have been forcibly removed.[10] Today, soil is being lost to sea level rise, to soil erosion through agricultural intensification, to contamination from industrial pollutants, to suffocation and terraformation accompanying the development of agricultural lands. It takes at least 500 years, and in many places thousands of years, to create an inch of topsoil absent human intervention.

How are our grammars, practices and expressions of the holy already shifting – and how must they now radically shift, as the ground shifts beneath us? I am decomposing the holy ground I once professed to stand upon, at the same time recognizing that the ground I stand upon is decomposing, holy. Decomposition is a consecration, a liturgy enacted by many human and more-than-human witness-participants, making desecrated ground capable of new life.

I do not seek to provide answers, but instead a prayer, one that asks how we can be formed into the kinds of earth-bound beings who might be prepared already for, and actively tending to, this ultimate fate of ours. I do not presume to know the end of the story. I resist that pathological hope for the destruction of those we profess to love. Our revelation is too murky for that, my prayer is too honest for that, our lives are too contingent for that. What partial revelations are available to us already, and how might these transform our practice and help to heal the damaged land from which our revelation derives? What happens to us when we do not know, distanced as we are from the knowedge of our ancestors who once knew how to survive here? What happens to us when we are not so certain anymore? What happens when we take a posture of humility, bending closer towards the humus, tuning our senses to this ground? What will we find there?

Notes

1 O'neil Van Horn, 2023, *On the Ground: Terrestrial Theopoetics and Planetary Politics*, Fordham University Press.

2 María Puig de la Bellacasa, 2017, 'Soil Times: The Pace of Ecological Care', in *Matters of Care: Speculative Ethics in More Than Human Worlds*, 3rd edn, University of Minnesota Press, pp. 169–216.

3 Esther 4.14.

4 David Foster Wallace, Barry Graham and Michael Korda, 'Tense Present: Democracy, English, and the Wars over Usage', *Harpers Magazine*, April 2001, pp. 39–58.

5 Kyle Powys Whyte, 2017, 'Our Ancestors' Dystopia Now: Indigenous Conservation and the Anthropocene', in Ursula K. Heise, Jon Christensen and Michelle Niemann (eds), *The Routledge Companion to the Environmental Humanities*, Routledge, pp. 222–31.

6 Donna Haraway, 'Anthropocene, Capitalocene, Plantationocene, Chthulucene: Making Kin', *Environmental Humanities* 6(1) (2015), pp. 159–65, https://doi.org/10.1215/22011919-3615934.

7 On climate change as a religious threat, see Willis Jenkins, 'Naturalized: White Settler Christianity and the Silence of Earth in Political Theology', *Political Theology Network*, 1 October 2018, https://politicaltheology.com/naturalized-white-settler-christianity-and-the-silence-of-earth-in-political-theology/, accessed 21.05.2025.

8 Wendell Berry, 2014, 'Manifesto: The Mad Farmer Liberation Front', in Wendell Berry and Ed McClanahan, *The Mad Farmer Poems*, Counterpoint, pp. 19–21.

9 Sallie McFague, 1993, *The Body of God: An Ecological Theology*, Fortress Press.

10 Whyte, 'Our Ancestors' Dystopia Now'.

I

Triangulating

Winter solstice

Deep winter is also the beginning of spring. In winter we inventory seeds, thumb through catalogues that stimulate our hunger and desire, and misremember the preceding year – diminishing its challenges, selecting memories of its beauty, and finding within us seeds of energy to take up the work again next season as our tired, baked bodies rest and heal. In the year's circular timeline, winter solstice is a meeting point where beginning and ending collide. Days indiscernibly lengthening are the first harbinger of a summer still a far-off figment.

Ground frozen, dormant, devoid of green and covered in snow, we make plans for a reality in which we've lost bearing, overestimating our capacity, underestimating the unexpected interfering in crop plans well laid. We retreat indoors and inward, left alone with an imagination to slowly regrow. Eventually, we romanticize again, misremembering the messiness, believing once again in our ability to overcome the inevitable limitations that pile up endlessly once the work begins in earnest. For now, the work is still and dreaming.

For now, the work is reacquaintance: coming again to know the place we are, weaving lessons learned from the work behind for the work before us. This is a time for reassessment, slowing down enough to reorient and reconsider our place in the world we inhabit. The season begins with this grounding, in the dark. Anything is possible beginning in a long winter.

Soil work

I am learning how to be a farmer, working, living and writing with stolen and degraded land, the ancestral home of the Lenni-Lenape, Lenapehoking. I do not belong to this land and this land does not belong to me. I am alienated from my own ancestry, following generations of emigrants who have run from land. I have run from the land, too: from the place I call home in the rocky, mountainous West, land of the Southern Arapaho. I have tended land and left land called *Azucsagna*. Ute land. Potawatomi land. Eno and Occaneechi land. I have shaped these lands and they have shaped me in return.

From each of these places, soils linger in my olfactory memory. Place has taste and texture my body moves through in tension or with ease. All these topographies are inhabited by more beings than my dulled senses can perceive. Their witness is recorded in the traces they leave in soil layers, time fossilizing, eroding.

In a moment of great and intensifying unease, uncovering old wounds is tedious and painstaking, requiring an attentiveness I am afraid I have lost. As these wounds, remembered, resurrect through soil, a timeline I thought ran only in one direction loops back. I am brought back, too, by older stories rising to surface through elevators of weathering. Matter: not created, never destroyed, always in movement, in me.

This soil is alive, ever animated by the breath of those divine. So too, soil is animated by labour, willing and forced. In the garden, the tines of digging forks gently uplift heavy and frequently saturated silt loam, a technique that alleviates compaction with a rush of oxygen, opening soil pores to receive more fully the gift of rain. For centuries here, our machines have crushed the intricate, spongey webs of life and cooperation that are the soil. Thinking soil a dead thing, Western minds, tools and ambitions have made it so.[1] It is the living who might lend soil a breath – our work and our care a form of resuscitation. Leaf-turned-litter decomposes in forest floors, slowly burying the sun's energy in photosynthesis fibres underground. Those still cycling the breath of life, earthworm and nematode, put their work there too, an offering.

Digging is a long process, from which distraction is a constant tug. The work happens slowly, slower than the quick conditioned pace of instant gratification. When I am away from the farm for more than a day, the pace of transformative growth is perceptible and astonishing. But in the work, its pace is ours, slow enough to evade detection. The visitor arrives in the garden with enthusiasm, revelling in a sudden beauty whose process they seldom understand, while those intimate with its creation know well its costs. Demanding the work of bearing food be done by migrant and alienated labourers makes its produce into a magic act. Fruits appearing on grocery shelves without explanation deceive us, as though the preceding processes involve no one. Outsourcing this labour absolves us of the responsibility to look, to see our own reflection in the mud.

This writing is an invitation to return to the ground to which we belong, where life and death hold together in vibrant and dynamic tension. This is an offering to repent of the destruction to which the soil bears witness – and more, to mend and repair torn relations with those who still offer us life. No more hollow assurances or misanthropic dreams that things will work out better when humans are gone; our disappearance is an impossibility. Our traces touch all earthly environments, now irreversibly and into eternity. Now we must learn what to do.

Disorientation (a history)

I was raised in a tradition bending towards a dangerous extremism, a tradition that has been an earth-destructive, political force couched in pious talk of reconciliation and some kind of healing I could never understand. What we were being reconciled *to* was rather ill-defined, always out of reach, never anything I could touch. I am becoming older now, in a climate destabilized, an environment polluted, plasticized and paved over, a world that is being and becoming trashed, struggling to breathe and lashing out. So too, I have shaped these lands, and they have shaped me in return.

I ask myself this question: is there something earth-destructive endemic to Christianity?[2] I have hoped for the recovery of a tradition now wholly enmeshed within the violence of right-wing extremism, white nationalism and patriotism, and fuelling allegiance to the settler state, hoping that fragments of a distorted narrative might yet be rearranged towards life-giving ends. Now, I am not so sure.

It is difficult to overestimate the insidiousness of a theological error I internalized very early: that this earth was not my home. This verdant, soft, pulsing earth that catches us at every moment, whose gravity draws us always to that place that gives us everything, was somehow fallen, broken beyond repair, unredeemable, already on course to burn. I conceived this fallen condition as given. It made me hope in something worse: the hope of that invented gospel, the one that rested on – and wrested – the earth's condemnation. Salvation was not the love that earth offers unconditionally in ongoing relation, but this relation's very severing.

With unapologetic argumentation and emotional manipulation, we sought to save converts from a world we called dark and to close them inside another dark world, not of moonless nights or subterranean mystery, but air-conditioned, unexceptional church buildings darkened at sunrise, erected from the refuse of capitalism's crises and already world-endings. Filling not old but already obsolete, greige concrete shopping centres where parking, at least, was abundant, we closed our eyes and experienced ourselves – god, ego, *cogito* – and insisted on reality's immateriality. The damage is still being done, daily, as more are dragged deeper into dissociation: unable to see daily actions – their costs, their consequences – for and with the soil. The haze of hatred, distraction and god talk is heavy in built environments deliberately obscuring dependence on what always and forever comes from and returns to earth. Enlisting soil in civilizing projects seeks salvation from a ground that endlessly upends, but turns this living ground into something more threatening to civilizations than before.

> 'Whosoever shall seek to save their life shall lose it, and whosoever shall lose their life shall preserve it.'[3]

What did it feel like for you when you came here the first time? What did this land, after so many miles of sea, feel like? What did it sound like, breathing, before sliced up, bisected and mined? How did the water move through it, before canals, dams and ditches made it go other ways? Where did you land, and who was there, witnessing? Who still witnesses you here? The land is alive, can you feel it? The land is not – was never – empty.

As one descended from Europeans, I wonder what they felt when they came. The power of a living, inhabited but unknown land threatened to undo them and unravel self-concepts derived from an old world subdued. Was it disdain, born of terror, in those self-selectively severed from the familiarity of home? Was it fear or ambition, then, that caused them to fabricate a new world in their image, an image that would otherwise have slipped away?[4]

When those with pale skin and a lust for mythologized comforts came to this place, they feared this so-called wilderness, this lush body of unrecognizable foods, medicines and paths. They cleared it, transforming and reconfiguring a new Europe.[5] They saw, desired and made this land as *tabula rasa*, lusting for the power to create a new Eden *ex nihilo*,[6] silencing what chirped and whirred and was so little understood. They cried *peace, peace* but there was no peace in the silence they contorted in the clearing.[7] This silence of the settler was not given but taken forcibly through genocidal violence, displacement, imperial expansion and extinction, both then and now. The silence of the land and skies emptied of bison and passenger pigeon is unsettling us now.[8]

Learning to listen

Learning to farm is learning to listen – to your body, the land and, in their interaction, the body of God.[9] Mine wilts readily in the thick, heavy heat the plants either love or hate. Farming is humbling, at times humiliating. To do that honourable work of bringing forth food from the land, you must know the ways of the plants – and each of them has a different way.

I cannot contain this unruly garden. The life of the soil bursts forth and germinates weeds sometimes taller and stronger than me. My arms tire trying to uproot lambsquarters, chenopod relative like the carrots I will tediously cultivate in their place, but which have adapted to establish early and without my help, gaining a foothold over the slower, more sensitive plants who have become accustomed to human coddling.[10] Weeds like these resist the predictability of harvest yields calculated by bed foot, yet nourish like spinach nonetheless.

My sore feet circle, and circle the garden again, trying clumsily and belatedly to adapt, observe patterns rapidly and memorize the lifeways of this one, small space. When I am at my limit, feeling alone in this mostly thankless effort, I understand the temptation of pesticides and plastic, polluting partners in a struggle *against* soil. To subdue the land is a temptation, conceptually simpler than the endless effort to dance clumsily with constant change. At best, farming is skilful cooperation with life, but our culture's systematic devaluation of this art form has made land's discipline and control expedient and necessary. 'The human grasp necessarily diminishes whatever it holds.'[11]

Fictions of individualism are a pervasive kind of sin. A lie that is being tested and tried by cascading paradigm shifts.[12] A lie being violently uprooted by successive climatic catastrophes in this geological moment, making us painfully aware that all our lives and actions are connected. A lie that keeps us acting as though our actions do not really matter – that is, have material consequence – that is, *make* matter. For all of us (not just us farmers) our actions move matter, rearranging the raw materials of the environments we increasingly construct. The lie that does not trace this mattering conceals the harm we manufacture and places impossible burdens on so many others yet unborn.

Individualism emerges from insecurity, but ultimately makes us more insecure. Individualism and white supremacy work to distance us from an earth that imposes limits – making the land a kind of dead thing, stripped of its power to challenge us or decompose us or feed us. To be fed, on the other hand, is a vulnerable act, requiring consent. Its implication is contingency, a fundamental fragility and dependence confronting the lie at the heart of individualism and supremacist logic. To eat is also to welcome transformations: to become with another, implying that I am not my own, implying that 'me' is a more complicated designation.

Letting supremacist logic keep its grip on us, we eschew our power to participate in the coming transformations, merely waiting, passively, for the end. If there will be an end at all, who can say, and what kind of end will that be? By some, this time has been called the Dithering:[13] a moment of collective moral abnegation. It is the unsettling ubiquity of underlying injustice alongside a cultural imperative to preserve it. This is my daily discomfort – mind and feet running, as if through quicksand, yet never arriving where I know I ought to be. The compromises pile up, obscuring the guiding vision. Am I running to or from something? I wonder. Frayed nerve endings limit reverence for life as my strategies for stability in an unstable world's ending begin to fail, one by one. Once self-protective, individualism now threatens my very existence. Forgetting my identity is constituted by ties that bind, I act as though my greatest power is in severing them. But biologically speaking, it is these ties that hold us together in the web of life. Ongoing relationship is not only life's prerequisite, but life's very definition. When do we start acting accordingly?

The religion of my upbringing glossed over this relationship, prioritizing that between disembodied souls and a disembodied deity. Divine image-bearers destined for eternal life, while the rest of the mortal world would pass away inconsequentially. We were taught not to trust our senses, idolators celebrating materiality unduly, harbouring ourselves with the like-minded, distancing ourselves from the supposedly profane. Growing older, ambition takes a parallel track, humming along with racist undertones, a quest to detach from dirty work and those skilled in it, to specialize and impose artificial distance from the many sources of our lives and their manual labour. The world of class-privileged knowledge-workers seems smooth and pleasant, but it is violent underneath, when our addictive devices connect us intimately with children in Congo who mine cobalt with bare hands. Those distanced from these pits live in fabricated worlds not so different from that celestial paradise, endlessly worshipping the eternality of endless growth. Our moral senses break across these spatial tensions. Relations of domination, though obscured and concealed, remain firmly intact, propped up by whiteness. Even those living in a heaven wrested from the ground will not escape it.

'Nature', subdued and manipulated, is quieter. City parks, ornamental trees and mowed lawns project airs of manageability, as if these arrangements were natural, as if this were what the land, where it is allowed to come up for breath between concrete streets and foundations, desires to be. Invisible labour always aids civilizing projects, as those rendered invisible exert countless hours to maintain a fabricated stasis – the pleasant environments in which pleasantries populate. Absent intense intervention, these fantasies fall away.

Nature, unmanageable, is getting loud. The alarms are sounding, shaking us awake, as more meddling cannot simply reverse centuries of mounting, positively reinforced impacts to ecosystems or walk us back from the brink of tipping points. This nature wasn't meant to be silenced.

Learning to farm is facing, struggling with and sometimes against the great power of life that is land. It is not always a pleasant experience, but one that frequently brings me to my knees and to tears. Yearly cycles of ambition are buried in the land, season after season, as I am continually reminded of my own finitude, dependence and mortality. Humbled by the recognition of the work it takes merely to make a salad, and the understanding that if it is not mine, it is someone else's, somewhere else, to do. I am addicted to this land work, though at times I think it might kill me.

Troubling landscapes

Some say agriculture is our species' original sin. They say ours was a fall *into* agriculture.[14] Today, dominant forms of agriculture could certainly be classified as a kind of sin against land. If we were to judge these cultural practices by their fruit, we would be troubled by a list of externalities that seem to endlessly multiply: not only deepening alienation from the source for our food, but worsening health crises, pollution and eutrophication, petrochemical dependence, plasticulture,[15] labour injustices, debt bondage, repackaged legacies of sharecropping, and more. Industrial agriculture reveals a pervasive dysfunction at its root – a sin that seeks to elevate the interests of some humans over those of all others, ever in pursuit of profits, efficiency improvements and godlike technologies that promise to loosen dependency's ties.

But even before agriculture's industrialization, the history of farming in the West was complicated and troubling. As certain agricultural worlds have been made, other worlds have been unmade or rendered invisible. Since the founding of the United States, yeoman farmer myths, homestead dreams and imperatives of enclosure have fuelled settler colonialism and capitalism on American frontiers, effecting ongoing exiles, dispossessions and the obliteration of countless life forms, whether directly to make way for those imported, or indirectly as a consequence.[16] As agriculturalists reshaped landscapes and watersheds by and for agriculture, they also altered patterns of life and cultural identity. What today seem wholly natural – sedentary lifestyles, land ownership and land's unceasing 'improvement' through agriculture, development and accompanying appreciations – are very recent shifts. It is these arrangements that have been utterly influential in the making of the modern human[17] – self-possessed, in control, individual.[18]

Agriculture in America is no neutral affair, and European agriculture, in concert with the plow and the Homestead Acts, has been integral to – indeed, remains the very mechanics of – land dispossession. Agriculture – accompanied by a particular kind of frontier dream and a fiction of homestead freedom still potent and prescient – has indelibly transformed the continent, turning it into parcelled property in our minds, maps and laws. 'Mixing land' with European labour has long been recognized and legitimized as the means of settler appropriation.[19] Homesteads still move through families justified by the state in their taking. It is these lands that continue to be transformed, eroded, poisoned and stripped of life to feed *this* world we cannot imagine living beyond. We insist we must 'feed the world'.[20] Rarely do we ask which one.[21]

The patterns of European agriculture reshaping this land and erasing its Indigenous presence continue to shape the way I work with it and the way I imagine transforming it still. I struggle to imagine the old forests felled to satisfy the felt needs of an insecure nation seeking a kind of omniscience in the clearing, trading the vast unknown for timber to build replica cities for a colony-turned-colonizer.[22] I can hardly imagine the innumerable bison ranging from the Great Plains to Appalachia. I realize that my failure of imagination was exactly the outcome sought by the murderous policy that aimed explicitly to transform an advanced, ecological agriculture adapted to this varied landscape – cooperative, migratory and symbiotic – into an agriculture patterned after that of another land. No landscape is natural,[23] and this land has been profoundly transformed through varied means: rapid deforestation, extermination, allotment and utopian visions effecting the transfer of stolen land in 160-acre parcels to those selected to become model citizens of a new nation. My land work follows this legacy, as I continue to effect its transformation.

While it has been profoundly reshaped and terraformed, the land also resists transformations born of violent simplification. Though malleable, living land is not infinitely so; it does not always cooperate with the plans of its shapers. Every soil, formed of bedrock and geological histories entirely unique to place, has its own pattern and form which do not always fit neatly inside the shape of imported desires. Cleared of anchoring trees to make vast plantations, fragile hillsides collapsed, and old soils eroded, washed out through gulleys. Cutting deeper and deeper, moving west, in search of waning tilth with increasingly militarized tools, homesteaders found the wind carried away the wealth of topsoil they sought. The bad habits of our agricultural predecessors – degrading and abandoning the land they touched on their way west to the Pacific – still support American myths of inexhaustibility, even as they exhaust.

Though the soil on which we stand has yet been buried, compacted, suffocated and perforated with vast networks of concrete corridors, roads and tunnels, this soil is still alive, and can be made more so. Like soils that form through layers of space in time, our existence is composed of those who came before us. We live through the matter of their ongoing. *Where* and *when* we are becomes the stuff of our bodies, the paths we walk make knots that create our lives.[24] Seeking to shape land in another image, the farmer finds her own image transformed. Fictions of fixity inscribed in property lines evade our grasp, seeping through the porous borders through which plants and animals freely move. The tighter the grip, the more slippery these evasions.

Working to transform the land, the cravings that propel the work hurt me. At times, I injure myself struggling to produce food in a way that is unnaturally solitary, a harsh but widespread reality when so few of us in so-called developed worlds do the work of food production. Farmers bear the burden of keeping neighbours fed – well, they hope – but receive little recognition. Most immigrant farm workers have no hope of belonging to the nation they feed, by design.[25] It is the fact that farming is such a profound responsibility, a public service coupled with feigned social invisibility, that turns me defensive.

Given the rules of the neoliberal economic environments constructed for us, it is difficult to make a living farming. The work has been hard all along, eating by the sweat of the brow,[26] but it is made harder in a culture programmed to extract from the ground more than it returns. Those who work intimately with and proximate to the ground know this extraction especially, and they share its physical and psychological consequences.[27] For some, the work's reward is enough to bear the costs. Making an honest living, a deeper living, to make living a possibility at all is a life-worthy sacrifice. Season after season, farmers stand the heartbreak and back-break for love, while their labour is devalued, misunderstood and never as automated as techno-utopian dreams of precision-agriculture's machines that only the most landed can afford would have us think.

Despite these inflated advancements, we still live in a world where the fruit of the land depends on cheapened but skilful manual labour, from strawberry fields to slaughterhouses. Few feel the weight and cost of this fact, when the products of the labour of lives swell landfills. When food is understood as a commodity, its purpose is not nourishment but achieving the highest price. Transforming living food into preservable products that make us sick, market forces ensure food fills shareholder portfolios before pantries or bellies. On both ends of fragile supply chains, there is hunger.

Decomposition

When I work in the garden, I oscillate between collusion with and resistance to agriculture's civilizing force, as I struggle to coax order out of chaos.[28] I locate competing desires at work in me. Obsessions with on-farm productivity – necessary for any hope of sustainable profitability – also drive wedges between human managers and the land that sustains our livelihoods. We treat the soils for which we care as machines, imposing a predictable ratio of inputs and outputs. A crop plan laid out linearly on a neat and tidy spreadsheet provides a god's-eye view of an operation that calculates the profitability of seed-borne life per linear foot. This is a convenient, even necessary simplification of a farm's true and utter unruliness – which, in doses too large, is a sure recipe for overwhelm. Long, sweaty July days do not lend themselves to peaceful contemplation in the fields, and too much rejoicing in too much floral and faunal wonder distracts from the day's urgent work.

At times, I derive satisfaction, even pleasure, in exerting a power that tames or slows the life of the garden which is at times too much to bear or comprehend. I remove weeds whose names I do not know but I'm told offer medicine. I sense achievement when looking upon a stale seedbed, though I know this euphemism – *stale* – is not only inaccurate but inhumane. I meditate on this and many other choices we make in the practice of an agriculture surely more sustainable, but inseparable from the compromised condition of our times. I know that my pleasure and my despair both reflect all I do not understand. I have been conditioned not only to exercise but to desire control and power over the incomprehensibly heterogeneous livings and their many meanings here.

There are many ways to care for soil. Though they may be taught and passed down, our land relations are not prescribed, but entirely open-ended. There are as many ways to tend a farm or garden as there are farmers and gardeners. When the Genesis story directs dominion, fruitfulness and multiplication, we read too much between the lines, assuming dominion to mean domination, multiplication to refer narrowly to the reproduction of human life, and our interpretation of these directions to be naturalized by divine ordination. But we multiply in a multiplicity of ways: propagating cuttings and rootstock, saving seeds, multiplying the many billions of soil microbial lives through the arrangement of welcoming habitat or brewing compost tea. Fertility, after all, refers to soil conditions, too.

Some farmers seek to mimic nature, proctoring experiments of minimal interference, harvesting the benefits of emerging plant collaborations and suffering the consequences of relinquished control. On the other end of the spectrum, control is a first guiding principle: control of seed genetics, plant pests and disease; this is agriculture more science than art.

Agriculture's human players may assume a variety of roles and job titles. A farm manager works for control and an efficient organization of labour: calculating labour costs by hours and inputs, and seeking to reduce these over time to improve profit margins. This is dominion in practice: the manager acting as a divinely ordained ruler who seeks to control the activity and trade of those within his kingdom while improving the productivity of the land.

A farmer might also identify as a steward of natural resources, and seek not to appropriate but to return the value that comes from partnering with land. Or perhaps the human plays the role of facilitator, brokering interactions between a system's disparate parts and players, bacteria and fungi to improve overall function. Any good rancher will describe themselves as a grass farmer, harnessing solar energy to feed the animals who improve the root zone and photosynthetic potential of prairie-adapted perennials. The meat that humans derive from these complex land-based interactions is merely a byproduct of a well-functioning ecosystem.

Perhaps the human is an organizer – listening deeply to the needs and desires of the individuals who constitute this community, and seeking to build coalitions and collaborations to meet a variety of goals: human food production being one among many, and not necessarily primary. An 'organizer' does not manage puppets but the inevitable messes that arise from the interaction between people and living systems, and within the systems themselves, seeking always to understand the needs and motivations of the various players interacting with one another on the scene. Good organizing requires attentiveness to multiple factors and actors and responds intelligently to those it follows.

We see the impacts of human intervention in every place we are lucky to know. How we respond to inherited impacts is our choice and our responsibility. The farm where I work was a sod farm before. The cultural practice here involved exporting not only the rhizomatic Bermuda grass (which still haunts this place in the heat of the summer) but the inches of topsoil in which its roots grew. Sod farming is notoriously extractive, and knowing this now causes me to see the lawns that line so many cities and suburbs differently: as pieced-together places made by many other places belonging to many others, hiding beneath the surface, these grass patches a Frankensteinian creation of soil commodification.[29] The grass here exerts a powerful inertia, living from the legacy of this place's prior management and its remaining rhizomes – creeping into carrot beds whose borders – like ours – are shown to be artificial by their permeability.

When working with degraded and contaminated soils, stories like these are always within reach. Stories of human–soil formation and soil–human formation are both as old as our species, though stories of intensifying soil deformation, disintegration or degradation are characteristic of this age of colonization, urbanization, globalization. This is the context we inherit, the geography we work inside (and against).

The degradation I inherit is manifold. Not only are the soils I daily work with physically, chemically and biologically degraded, but so too is my vision of soil life. For as much as I am learning about the liveliness of soils, preconceptions of soil as a dead instrument – a tool – still need to be unlearned. My imagination of control and good management is still marked by the degradation of imagination: that human–soil formation is driven and controlled by our species, when I know the process is mutual at best.

When I work in the garden, I consider the winding road that led me to this place. To this set of desires, and the compromises I have made to enlist myself in the most basic of vocations – soil care. Though by no means easy, this work is the definition of downward mobility, bringing me closer than is comfortable to my own nothingness – right where I began. I am caked in dust by the end of a long day, the soil that covers my every inch and orifice prophesying my death already. And yet, to be brought this close to the death that touches resurrection is a continual gift, feeding my simple imagination which would unnecessarily bifurcate these. Every done day is a homecoming to the soil, my doing and undoing. This, I remember, is all I am meant to be.

I once had great ambitions for my life. Now I see the meaning of life as more pliable, more momentary: to enjoy and to share the fruit of shared labour, to make food with one another, to survive.[30] Perhaps the meaning of life is not hidden inside the mind as some attitude or outlook, but in our making and maintaining of food-bearing environments that come to bear better attitudes or outlooks in time. Perhaps we have what we need already, in bread that joins the love and labour of many to sustain the life many might love.

But just as grain growing and wild yeast feeding, making bread, becoming food, becoming compost, becoming soil, attest to an eternality less like that heavenly stasis (a forever that always terrified me) and more like everyday ongoing, there is another kind of eternality facing us in this time some call the Anthropocene. Eternal artefacts (some) relentlessly manufacture, (more) use momentarily, insist upon living with (all of) us forever. The plastic I find in this soil, growing alongside my food, imposes itself unwelcome in the soil profile via the leaf mulch picked up from the nearby road, repurposed here. Its bright colours and sharp, flashing pieces leave me under no illusion that this environment is 'natural'. That figure of the human – *anthropos* – which still excludes so many of us, this ravenous monster insisting on endless growth,[31] is a soil-forming factor, too. The monster leaves marks, traces upon the surface of the soil, reworked too by machines and plant companions – and in oceans, plastistones.[32]

Grounding: a prayer

Though I struggle to see in the dark, this struggle is my first step. The work of my hands touches stories that trouble, and yet they are mine to rework. When soil sleeps and days are short, it is patience I need, while the work is ahead and behind.

Notes

1 In *Desert Notebooks*, Ben Ehrenreich writes that our seeing affects our treatment of the earth (as a thing). Ben Ehrenreich, 2021, *Desert Notebooks: A Road Map for the End of Time*, Counterpoint.

2 Lynn White, 'The Historical Roots of Our Ecologic Crisis', *Science*, 155, no. 3767 (March 10, 1967): 1203–7.

3 Luke 17.33.

4 See Willie James Jennings, 2010, *The Christian Imagination: Theology and the Origins of Race*, Yale University Press.

5 For a discussion on the way in which agriculture and colonization created 'Neo-Europes', see Amitav Ghosh, 2022, *The Nutmeg's Curse: Parables for a Planet in Crisis*, University of Chicago Press, p. 52.

6 Whitney A. Bauman, 2007, 'Creatio Ex Nihilo, Terra Nullius, and the Erasure of Presence', in Laurel Kearns and Catherine Keller (eds), *Ecospirit: Religions and Philosophies for the Earth*, Fordham University Press, pp. 353–72.

7 Teagan Steele-Fisher, 2019, *Apost(le)ate*, self-published, p. 58.

8 William Cronon, 2003, *Changes in the Land: Indians, Colonists, and the Ecology of New England*, Hill and Wang, a division of Farrar, Straus and Giroux (first published 1983).

9 Sallie McFague, 1993, *The Body of God: An Ecological Theology*, Fortress Press.

10 Michael Pollan, 2002, *The Botany of Desire: A Plant's-Eye View of the World*, Random House.

11 Wendell Berry, 2009, preface to Masanobu Fukuoka, *The One-Straw Revolution: An Introduction to Natural Farming*, New York Review of Books, p. xiv.

12 See Aminah Al-Attas Bradford, 'Religion, Animals, and the Theological Anthropology of Microbes in the Pandemicene', *Religions*, 13(12), 1146 (December 2022), https://doi.org/10.3390/rel13121146.

13 Donna Haraway, 'Anthropocene, Capitalocene, Plantationocene, Chthulucene: Making Kin', *Environmental Humanities*, 6(1) (2015), pp. 159–65, https://doi.org/10.1215/22011919-3615934, citing Kim Stanley Robinson, 2012, 2312, Orbit.

14 S. Lily Mendoza, 2018, 'Composting Civilization's Grief: Life, Love, and Learning in a Time of Eco-Apocalypse', in Eileen R. Tabios (ed.), *Humanity: An Anthology, Volume 1*, Paloma Press, pp. 118–36. See also Wes Jackson, 1980, *New Roots for Agriculture*, University of Nebraska Press.

15 Jessica Feeser, Gladis Zinati and Jeff Moyer, 2014, 'Beyond Black Plastic: Cover Crops and Organic No-Till for Vegetable Production', Rodale Institute, 2014, https://rodaleinstitute.org/education/resources/beyond-black-plastic/, accessed 06.06.2025.

16 For example, the brucellosis between bison and cattle, or the spread of pneumonia from domesticated to bighorn sheep herds.

17 See Sylvia Wynter, 'Unsettling the Coloniality of Being/Power/Truth/Freedom: Towards the Human, After Man, Its Overrepresentation – An Argument', *CR: The New Centennial Review*, 3(3) (2003), pp. 257–337.

18 Willie James Jennings, 2020, *After Whiteness: An Education in Belonging*, Wm. B. Eerdmans Publishing.

19 John Locke, 1821, 'Chapter V. Of Property' in *Two Treatises of Government*, Whitmore and Fenn, pp. 208–30.

20 David E. Bell, Carin-Isabel Knoop and Mary Shelman, 2009, rev. 2012, 'Monsanto: Helping Farmers Feed the World', Harvard Business School, https://www.hbs.edu/faculty/Pages/item.aspx?num=38245, accessed 09.07.2025.

21 Ed Roberson, 2012, *To See the Earth Before the End of the World*, Wesleyan University Press.

22 Frieda Knobloch, 2000, *The Culture of Wilderness: Agriculture as Colonization in the American West*, University of North Carolina Press.

23 William Cronon, 'The Trouble with Wilderness: Or, Getting Back to the Wrong Nature', *Environmental History* 1(1) (1996), pp. 7–28, https://doi.org/10.2307/3985059.

24 Tim Ingold describes placemaking as knot tying: 'Proceeding along a path, every inhabitant lays a trail. Where inhabitants meet, trails are entwined, as the life of each becomes bound up with the other. Every entwining is a knot, and the more that lifelines are entwined, the greater the density of the knot.' Tim Ingold, 2011, 'Against Space: Place, Movement, Knowledge', in *Being Alive: Essays on Movement, Knowledge and Description*, Routledge, pp. 145–55.

25 Seth M. Holmes and Jorge Ramirez-Lopez, 2023, *Fresh Fruit, Broken Bodies: Migrant Farmworkers in the United States, Updated with a New Preface and Epilogue*, University of California Press.

26 Genesis 3.19.

27 Deborah B. Reed and Deborah T. Claunch, 'Risk for Depressive Symptoms and Suicide Among U.S. Primary Farmers and Family Members: A Systematic Literature Review', *Workplace Health & Safety*, 68(5) (2020), pp. 236–48, https://doi.org/10.1177/2165079919888940.

28 For agriculture as civilization, see Lisa Wells, 2021, *Believers: Making a Life at the End of the World*, Farrar, Straus and Giroux.

29 Salvatore Engel-Di-Mauro and Levi Van Sant, 2020, 'Soils and Commodification', in Juan Francisco Salazar, Céline Granjou, Matthew Kearnes, Anna Krzywoszynska and Manuel Tironi (eds), *Thinking with Soils: Material Politics and Social Theory*, Bloomsbury Publishing, pp. 55–70.

30 Chris Newman, 2024, *First Generation Farming*, Sylvanaqua Farms.

31 Winona LaDuke and Deborah Cowen, 'Beyond Wiindigo Infrastructure', *South Atlantic Quarterly*, 119(2) (2020), pp. 243–68, https://doi.org/10.1215/00382876-8177747. See also Robin Kimmerer, 2013, 'Windigo Footprints', in *Braiding Sweetgrass: Indigenous Wisdom, Scientific Knowledge and the Teachings of Plants*, Milkweed Editions, pp. 303–9.

32 Liuwei Wang and Deyi Hou, 'Plastistone: An Emerging Type of Sedimentary Rock', *Earth-Science Reviews*, 247, 104620 (December 2023), https://doi.org/10.1016/j.earscirev.2023.104620.

2

Making *terra nullius*

Spring equinox

As winter's hold breaks from movements below ground, dormant seeds jolt awake in freeze–thaw oscillations. We have grown accustomed to the slowness, so much as to almost believe winter's contractions were a permanent state of lifelessness. The first signs of spring break the illusion when, after months of perceived stagnation, we are again reoriented to the aliveness of the world. Something stirs within us, too; it is time to catch up.

Land work is all about context. Land catalogues moments in time. Land work is attentive to these. Our land work is layered with the work of many others – human and more-than-human. We inherit the consequences of the actions of all those who precede us, not our own. And yet, it is ours to respond. All the same, our actions will determine and delimit those of those who follow. Land is no tabula rasa, but time, light and seasons, distilled.

It is not just our actions and desires that shape land, for we act alongside, following and preceding many. We find ourselves constrained by those with whom we share space and those whose time shaped the space we now share. This same land bears the marks of those who attempted to exert a will on a land unknown – those who forgot the context they lacked, inward-looking as they were. When they came colonizing and Christianizing this land they wanted tabula rasa, they saw terra nullius. What they could not see, at the time, they mistook for lack, setting to work to remake this land in the image of the European lands of which they were dispossessed, lands they misremembered and desired to bring about anew ex nihilo[1] in a new-to-them world.

In spring, our expectations meet reality, our ambition our limitation. As life wakes, its control slips from our fingers. Land has *agency – of this we are reminded each spring – in excess of our simplifications that seek understanding and fixity enough to control. We can work in concert or in conflict with life, but we can never control its unfolding.*

Making soil

To farm is to make soil – that thin skin of the earth that is the nexus between bedrock and atmosphere[2] – with critters and leftovers, time and temperature, water and strategy. What and how we eat erodes or builds the universe of soil under our feet, depending on how we manage the flows. Farming, then, is a process of changing a world and transforming environments, making them sites of nourishment or sacrifice zones.[3] Within given microclimates and topographies, a farmer creates a world emergent from that point at which vision and limitation meet. Agriculture is a generalist's discipline – and many disciplines in truth. A farmer is not only a farmer but also a botanist, entomologist, pathologist and genetic engineer, and functions as an accountant, carpenter, electrician, plumber and mechanic from one day to the next. If you've known a good farmer, you've no doubt seen this subtle brilliance – edges of earned intelligence smoothed by the daily, humbling recognition of land's ever-greater wisdom. Good farmers spend their lives learning to cooperate with the land, and learn lessons when shortsighted or defiant.

In a time of climate change, disruption and breakdown, the land is shouting its lessons louder. Those who work with land to feed us are sounding the alarm. While change has forever been the constant, governing impulse that maintains our continuity, patterns and rates of change are now changing too fast for our cognition to catch. As our language, governments and economies struggle to adapt, so too, entrenched patterns of settled agriculture resist the change that is already here. The ground we presumed to stand upon is now shifting under our feet. In many ways, we've asked for this.

Farmers are on the front lines of climate change – weathering the worst of the storms and heatwaves that are becoming more intense each season. We try in vain to save our animals from rising waters[4] and watch farmers plaster mud on tunnel walls to deflect the solar energy they once sought to harvest as novel heat domes sit and stay. Avian flu infects cattle while farmers canoe through a flooded Intervale, marking anniversaries of last year's 500-year deluge. In dryer places, those hell-bent on maintaining wealth manufactured by fallacies of endless growth shuttle water from farms towards growing cities, or hoard land for commoditized water, preying on vulnerable farmers who could lose everything in one more dry year. In many ways, we've asked for this.

Farming is a public service, performed by less than 2 per cent of the eating population, but the forms of agriculture that the US has condoned are not innocent. In the American West, agriculture is a mechanism of colonization,[5] where irrigators parted waters, incarcerated streams[6] and drained wetlands, transforming life-giving water into hay for cattle. Cows fed the miners who followed trappers and emulated their extractivism, polluting the soils and waters that still feed us all with heavy metals and acid mine drainage. Agriculture has been similarly extractive – mining fragile soils, exploiting public land, and codifying water as settler property.[7] Settlers transformed this Eden with imported tastes – for beef, displacing buffalo; for wheat, a holier sacrament than corn,[8] then corn commodified beyond recognition. The plow and the Homestead Acts, these technologies of land dispossession, still traffic in frontier fantasies perpetually parcelling properties. But the plow brought the dust bowl; the cows, cheatgrass; and reclamation, scarcity. Now, we are running out of the time ancient topsoil embodies,[9] and the West is a tinderbox.

Terraformation

Cultures make soil, and soils make cultures. Food cultures capture earth's *terroir*, reflecting and adapting to the soils from which they grow. But the soils a culture makes, and the cultures emergent from soils, are not as fixed as nationalists or their racist origin stories would hope,[10] not contained by artificial boundaries of *Blut und Boden*.[11] Seismic shifts and changing climates change soils and cultures too fast for nativists and their territorial tactics to recover. Soils accumulate novel contaminants, then wash down rivers in mudslides, which again reshape soil reshaped. Matter is *mater* before territory,[12] not inert but emergent, as generative as destructive, receiving and absorbing our care and our blows, returning the same – and always stronger.

Pedology is a name for the study of soils. As in pedestrian or pedon. As pedestrian footprints impress themselves upon the soil they tread, so building footprints and tyre marks disturb and reshape soil profiles. Soil pedons – units of soil held in your palm – come apart along fault lines carved by their inhabitants' exudates. A healthy, living soil therefore has *structure*, the structure made of movements of differently shaped creatures. The paths they carve make way for others – plant roots following worm tunnels, finding a gentler way to water and a trail of nourishment – castings like breadcrumbs they follow in the dark.

Human lifeways, like worm ways, change soil's shape and structure. Humans, too, make paths for plant lives. While earthworms excel at the finer tasks at which our scale makes us clumsy, we can do the heavier lifting: importing large quantities of organic matter from other sources to accelerate soil building. But our power is also our liability, our gift our responsibility.[13] Our size and technologies can do great harm – compacting soil and depleting its structure, expelling oxygen from its lungs and diminishing porosity, making soil sponges brittle, unable to hold the water they need to sustain the life they contain. Changing climates, the capital-driven activity of humans, cause mudslides and earthquakes – soil-building activities at scales that exceed our comprehension.

Our soils are anthropogenic. *Anthropedogenesis*: a made-up word for the processes by which the aggregated impacts of humans form soils,[14] though we know soils shape humans the same. Of the five 'soil-forming factors' – parent material, topography, time, temperature and biology – recognized by pedologists, humans seem to play but a small role. We are, to be sure, in company with other biological soil-forming factors, but our actions are now powerful in other ways, in partnership with technology, information and godlike machines. Humans may now be a sixth soil-forming factor – re-engineering topographies, mixing media derived from diverse locations and bedrock, altering soil biology with deadly chemicals and tampering with the temperature of the globe.[15]

Humans are soil people and always have been: made from soil, and making soil still. Humans are soil-makers inevitably, but *not* inevitably extractive or destructive against it. Infamously, Amazonian soils named *terra preta* turned red, iron-rich, tropical soils dark with the charcoal of generations living in and adapted to place. Soils are formed by the activity of so many humans and contain their traces over time. These soils formed of human habit – cooking and discarding charred waste, burning plants and returning carbon to the ground, containing bone and pottery shards to yield deep deposits of organic matter, building the fertility they need in places where topsoil would be thin without human intervention.

Human activity can build soil fertility, but it also depletes soil fertility, of course. Toxic soils, too, are anthropogenic. Industrial manufacturing and mining yield soils high in heavy metals. Even lead from car engines remains in soil decades later, resurfacing in our kids. Throughout history, humans have made soil, the byproducts of their living migrating down soil profiles – composted food scraps, wood ash, manure from ruminants and sapiens alike. They say no place on earth is untouched by humans now. Perhaps no soil on earth was ever untouched.

Prayer plows

Perhaps no technology has been as destructive to soils as the plow.[16] Earlier American settlers, instructed to 'venerate the plow',[17] vested it with a mythic power the yeoman farmer would wield. The plow would go on to shape the American continent in the image of another. Jethro Wood's moldboard plow and those that followed with ever deeper cuts dismembered soils, slicing through horizons and churning ancient layers into an erodible pulp. In defiance of the desert, settlers moving west tilled soils to dust, believing the rain would follow the plow.[18] Modern plows and discs more thoroughly rip apart fungal webs through which plants make and share soil food.[19] They tear through the food webs that sustain soil endlessly, making impaired soils dependent on outside chemical interventions. Turning over prairie soils formed by bison herds and deep-rooted perennials,[20] the plow turned prairie into homestead into dustbowl in pursuit of some manifest destiny, relentlessly seeking an ever-elusive improvement while sacrificing the conditions of eternal life already here.[21] Founding fathers imagined the plow would bring, if not a kingdom, an ideal republic made of those allied with its power over others. Indeed, as a heavier plow drove divisions deeper into soil, it also deepened divides along gendered lines, confining gendered-female agricultural labour indoors, to the reproductive, preservative and enclosed, and affixing masculine associations to increasingly warlike machinery that sought earth's subduction.[22]

The plow is a kind of prayer: the wedding of word and deed, a technology through which the word of manifest destiny became violent against flesh. The plow is an answer to a prayer for control and uniformity, used to lighten the load of agricultural labour, but now compromising the ground of agriculture's survival, and ours. The plow's prayer was kingdom come, but the answer came unexpectedly.

The plow looks towards the future and anticipates its arrival, erasing unruliness to make clean seedbeds for next season's crops. But just as it can save time forming a seedbed, it can accelerate degradation. Soils formed over millennia swept away in an instant windstorm or flash flood lost time in another sense. Soil disturbance now unsettles the certainty that subduction sought. Advocates of soil conservation now shun the plow, and more and more who know better now limit its use. Even those who deny climate change think soil conservation is patriotic. When land is territory, the loss of topsoil registers as a national security threat. Reducing disturbance, or tillage, is one of the golden rules for improving soil health, alongside cover cropping and crop rotation. Leaving soil undisturbed allows its connective tissue to regrow, as it would on a forest floor through the slow decomposition of organic matter depositions, becoming home to a biodiverse community of creatures adapted to place, making the place of soil suitable for their adaptation. When soil is allowed to be slow, slimy exudates create structure, as mechanical and chemical activity breaks down soil's composite parts to make food for a wide range of underground inhabitants. Soils undisturbed for long enough require fewer inputs, as soil creatures, eating and being eaten, break down and make available to plants all necessary nutrients from the bedrock and parent materials from which soils form.[23] Absent the disturbance of the plow, this kind of soil management mimics the slower soil-formation processes that protect the soil biodiversity responsible for soil structure, which is incidentally the best erosion control.[24]

As the plow's use anticipates the future, it unearths old stories and long-buried lives relegated to a forgotten past, overturning objects complicating descriptions of land as merely an input in harvest's yield. When this farm's soil was turned over for agriculture, plows turned over artefacts, testifying to this land's care for Lenape hunters who walked between the two great rivers across Lenapehoking, before immigrants were forced to dig canals to divert their waters into nodes of Mannahatta. What drew the animals drawing hunters to this low land is the same thing that later drew the farmers to the periphery of fledgling cities, and still draws the migratory birds I greet: alluvial soils replenished by streams. A boy, I'm told, followed the plows that turned dairy pasture into soil-exporting sod farm before its suburban development. He spotted sharp and shining arrowheads easily when the soil was worked and wet.[25] I think about that wet soil cut open, a violent disturbance with long-term consequences, bringing buried histories to the surface on its way somewhere else. I wonder what histories lie buried beneath the soil I do my best to leave undisturbed.

As a farmer I have disturbed my fair share of soil. I have disturbed soil even at the wrong time, when soil is too wet or compacted or too dry to be worked on a windy day. I once drove the tractor to the field cursing a rainstorm that had already begun, refusing to be set back three drying days. I have run a plow through the fleshy bodies of earthworms as they work diligently – if more slowly – to create the friable seedbed my plow seeks. Plowshares, still swords.

When I first came to this place, all I saw was a garden in winter, frozen and quiet. What I heard was an invitation: 'Do you think you can do something with this?' What I misunderstood at the time was that the land was a story – one I was entering, and late. Considering the many actors who made this place what I would encounter, my influence would be small. Though I desired a blank slate, a *tabula rasa*, to be terraformed into my mind's image, the land was not endlessly pliable. It had limits, constraints and history. I could do something with this, but only do *well* on this half-acre[26] insofar as I respected these.

Terra nullius and the Doctrine of Discovery

Christian teaching, practice and liturgy cannot exist apart from the land. The elements that animate the table and clothe celebrants are derived from land, after all. We say these elements are made holy by spirit, but they are transformed by the work of unseen others, too – weavers, yeasts and soil microbes, humans and their machines all play a role in making bread and wine spiritual food. The work of the spirit is tied to the work of the soil. Perhaps they are one and the same.

Christians are waking up to this, paying better attention to their land's deep history and recovering land's acknowledgement in ritual and teaching. They are moving outside, restoring habitat, and digging out old liturgies marking planting and harvest, and celebrating feast days of forgotten farmer-saints.

The Church has long taken land for granted. Land granted by monarchs vested with divine authority made churches believe the land was God's gift to them for the care of the parishes they served. But the land that was given was also land stolen. Land is now the largest source of wealth for many churches. Churches losing members are land rich but cash poor. At a moment when churches face existential threats, letting go of the land would spell ruin, but holding on to the land perpetuates a disturbing legacy.

The Doctrine of Discovery, a series of papal bulls penned in

1452 under Pope Nicholas V, established the legal and religious justification for Europeans to colonize the Western hemisphere, seize Indigenous lands, violently dispossess of their lands those deemed heathens, pagans, unbelievers and enemies of Christ, and 'reduce their persons to perpetual slavery'.[27] The Doctrine of Discovery sought to justify the taking and the violence that would ultimately benefit the monarchies of Spain, Portugal and later other colonial powers. Land theft and violence would advance the Christian gospel, they claimed.

The Doctrine of Discovery is not ancient history. It was not repudiated by the Catholic Church until 2023, and it remains the theological justification for colonial land relations all over the world. The doctrine upholds legal precedent for land dispossession. It was cited in a United States Supreme Court case denying the Oneida Nation ancestral lands in 2005.

It is a modern manifestation of colonialism to claim as gift that which was not given, but violently wrought by unholy alliances. A colonial habit, too, to imagine land as lifeless property, without inhabitants.

Terra nullius, the myth of land's emptiness, has long been a fiction powerful to dispossess. *Terra nullius* described lands supposedly belonging to no one – not uninhabited, but empty of any *Christians* with legitimate claim to that land. *Terra nullius* rendered invisible the caretakers of the land who made it the lush and navigable 'wilderness' colonists encountered.[28] Their work, too, was made invisible, like the work of those who maintain today's roads with great effort, but who are invisible until they are blamed for the potholes that interrupt traffic. The product of the labour of the invisible was called natural and primeval. 'Unimproved' wilderness: unremarkable and unproductive.[29] Fictions of *creatio ex nihilo* were imposed on the land, making nothing of its co-creators.[30]

It was Christians who called this land empty, saw this land empty and attempted to *make* this land empty of those they dehumanized. It is this same land from which the Church today prays. Our prayer is uttered from the taking, and has made this misunderstood land lifeless as a result. *Terra nullius* is a potent political vision, permission and prophesy.

Naming land, claiming land

If our actions make land, our words do the same. If humans are a factor forming soils, our language is one way in which we make them. A self-fulfilling prophecy turned *terra nullius* fictions into present realities, turning living land into dirt devoid of life, as a crisis of biodiversity now threatens soils that have always been constituted by their living members. What we call land affects how we see land, and then how we go on to shape the land we see. Our words make land as much as the work of our hands.

Robin Kimmerer writes that 'names are the way we humans build relationships, not only with each other but with the living world'.[31] She is concerned we do not know the names of plant relatives that offer us their food and medicine. The scientific names that work to catalogue species are not the same as the names that come with stories and instructions. Naming exerts a refractive power, like an optometrist's phoropter that makes legible what was initially incomprehensible. Naming enables recognition, the first step to understanding, and yet the words we use to name the world around us impact how we understand our responsibilities in it and how we relate to it.

Those who remember and recite creation myths know the power contained in words. Words are potent to transform land: in the beginning it was the Word that moved waters to define land's borders against seas. Today, another word – of deed and title – defines land's borders the same. As words shape worlds, praying shapes believing.[32] How we *pray* land affects how we see land, and how churches go on to shape the land they own and occupy. The *Book of Common Prayer* describes land as a resource producing wealth: 'Bless our land with honourable industry ... that every one of us may enjoy a fair portion of the riches of this land.'[33] Through industry, Mormon settlers shaped deserts into promised lands they called Moab, Eden and Zion,[34] irrigation projects making real prophesies that the desert bloom as a rose.[35]

Renaming can be a violation, erasing old stories to replace them with new ones. Amitav Ghosh writes: 'renaming was one of the principal instruments with which colonists erased the prior meanings of conquered landscapes', transforming them into new

Europes.³⁶ The 'new' in New York and New England is a word 'invested with an extraordinary semantic and symbolic violence', erasing and superimposing a vision to be achieved.³⁷ The new, Christian names given to children in boarding schools were likewise an exercise of dominance to remake and to control.

Colonial names still haunt the places those names touched.³⁸ That infamous European bore the name of his empire's god-man – *Christophus* – and spread his name from Columbia to Columbus, like the dove, *colombe*, who promised peace after endless miles of drowning sea. But this man and those who followed came bearing magnanimity's opposite – called upon a god victorious through empire. Many would follow this bearer of an imperial god to his 'new' world and make it so, renaming lands *terra nullius* to reclaim them for another.

Land as property

What do you think, when you think *land*?³⁹ Perhaps land is synonymous with soil, or dirt, or open space or vista. Maybe you read landscape like a page, tracing contour lines, peaks and valleys to find a passage to freedom. Or perhaps land for you denotes another kind of freedom – the freedom to own a small piece of it you might fence, from which you can exclude others, within which you can increase your net worth.⁴⁰

I was raised thinking land was this kind of thing – whether someone else's property or an otherwise bordered political boundary to which I belonged. In history books describing battles over land, land was merely a location among many others, and sometimes contested territory. The land might be beautiful or moving or evoke some nostalgia – but nonetheless belonged to a story tying land's ownership and development to imperatives of human progress, itself a kind of salvation *from* land's limitations. For some, land's development still registers as redemption from an unfriendly wild towards a quieting stability which predictably creates wealth for those able to overcome the societal vulnerability of landlessness. For many, we see land's value as it is measured in cash.

In a culture and economy built on the conversion of stolen land into real estate, it's easy to see land as property. Land's privatization is so totalizing, it can be near-impossible to see land any other way. Laws uphold the rights of possession, control, enjoyment, exclusion and the disposition of private property, even when adverse impacts spill over property lines. The practices of religious institutions regarding their properties reflect similar sensibilities – that the land to which they hold title is an asset to be managed. But is it possible for religious language to yield new practices that refute this dominant view, prioritizing land justice and treating land not primarily as a commodity, but in the uniqueness of its variability?

In my home place, where the Great Plains abut the Rocky Mountains, land is where earth meets sky and landscape extends in every direction, dotted with human habitation, dense and sparse according to its difficulty. In this continent's east, hemmed in by the Atlantic and Blue Range but once continuous with north Africa, soils are old and long weathered from underlying bedrock. The shoulders of the mountains are soft and spongey where leaf mould covers rich deposits of organic matter, built of decomposed leaves over many millennia. The land is hospitable to farming, also to the bugs who enjoy the same conditions.

In the West the story is different. Dramatic mountains, soaring to high and thin-aired elevations, rise abruptly out of the landscape, as they rose abruptly between fault lines and volcanic activity. These mountains and soils have not been so weathered. Plants here grow slowly and smaller, but stronger against the intense sun. In the West, land is big and beautiful, but brittle. Settlers here survive in spite of the land's constraints. Dreams of planned cities and plat maps grow dusty where water proved wanting. Communities fight to irrigate where not enough flows. Meanwhile, desert cities suck snowmelt from peripheral farms and food from further afield.

Still, in all their variability, these places have become property, obscuring underlying relations. The language of property flattens all this as it commodifies land: noting land's differentiating features only to determine the land's relative market value. *Terra nullius* lands were made property when land 'belonging to no one' was brought under cultivation and claimed by those the Church recognized, flattened in much the same way, brought under the control of religious language to tame the incomprehensible.

Land as resource

In our culture, land is capital, a resource to be mobilized in the making of other resources. Farmland especially has been financialized.[41] The already-wealthy increasingly pursue land as a stable investment, driving housing crises and the growing issue of agricultural land access. Even degraded land appreciates in this economy, as land's capacity for growth has little to do with its growing market value. Anyone who has been displaced by gentrification knows that what makes land values grow exponentially has more often to do with the 'laws' of scarcity and competition than land's other productive capacities – making clean air as it supports photosynthetic scrubbers, clean water as it absorbs and percolates rainfall to replenish groundwater, or topsoil that cycles biomass to yield food – though this can help.[42]

We derive so many resources from land, we've become comfortable describing land as a resource. In addition to oil and gas, metals and minerals, and other commodities, land-based resources include the immaterial. Conserved land is a now-scarce resource, islands of biodiversity and green space where proximate land has been degraded or developed. Real estate prices reflect the recreational value of public land resources and nearby mountains, replacing the value of mined minerals that drew prospectors a century ago, but still a form of mining, some say.[43] Land's spiritual value can be harder to protect against powerful energy lobbies.[44] To whom sacred land matters *matters* – and failing to defend land's value in market terms can cause those who resist land's propertization to lose fights against 'energy independence'. Quantifying a land's 'ecosystem services' to accurately account for the benefits that human economies derive from free 'natural resources' can help, but it also reduces land's value to the resources mobilized in human production and consumption, by putting a price on the priceless.[45]

Whether our education is formal or not, we are all trained as economists, accepting certain laws of behaviour and conforming our activities to them. We are wise or poor stewards of our time. We calculate the impacts of our actions to increase economic security. We know and navigate scarcity. We manage for abundance. We invest where we expect the best returns. Through all these activities, we have learned to be managers who control the flow of resources.

Environmental economists will argue that property ownership promotes stewardship. We are more motivated to preserve and enhance land's value when the profits are ours, they say. In the tragic telling, the commons are quickly exploited by individuals seeking to maximize their gain, and though this thinking has been contested, disproven, and shown to have racist origins and implications, it still profoundly impacts the way we see the world and our responsibilities in it.[46] We see the care of the commons not as an opportunity but as a liability, cooperation not as a calling but as an inconvenience.

Stewardship is a word for land care that is growing in use. It connotes the idea that we are not so much owners of a lifeless property or managers of a mechanistic landscape as participants in a complex ecology that demands our active and attentive care. Stewardship leaves what it finds better for the encounter. It seeks not to extract, but to grow the natural resources and productive potential of a place. For Christians, stewardship stands in contrast to damaging interpretations of dominion for which the Church is blamed.[47] Religious leaders attempt to reframe property rights as responsibilities. They describe the Church's calling as stewarding rather than exploiting the world God made. But stewardship leaves property relations mostly undisturbed, and reinforces the idea that land is a resource or storehouse of resources given to the Church for its benefit. Often, those who 'steward' land still treat it as an asset or investment, and good stewardship as that which protects land's financialized value. Churches steward their land in much the same way they steward financial resources, selling land assets to fund pensions and salaries. When the Church participates in an economy in which land is property, land stewardship grows the value of the land it holds, but not much else.

Natural resources are managed according to the same logic. A natural resource manager seeks not only the conservation but also the regeneration of land-derived resources, as does a regenerative farmer. As we march dangerously towards ecological overshoot, when earth's resources are consumed faster than they are regenerated and wastes are produced faster than they break down, correcting the trend of ecological destruction is imperative for human survival.[48] But the solutions we pursue are too often held captive by the logic of private property and resource extraction, even if the resources we value have changed. We protect places that are resource rich while degrading other places in equal measure: offsets seek balance in carbon accounting, but permit the degradation and pollution of so many backyards.

I manage the farm and its natural resources in this way: minimizing costs (of time, effort and costly inputs) to maximize savings, while preserving scarce resources. I invest energy savings where I believe they will bear fruit, cautiously avoiding time expenditures where I fear my effort may be lost. We invest in our soil continuously over time, trusting it will yield returns. A farm that seeks profitability is managed like other financial assets. We manage flows of solar energy, intensifying then waning throughout the season bookended by equinoxes, perforated by solstices. We direct this fluctuating solar energy down roots into soil, feeding life below ground. As the days lengthen, life in the above world in its chaos abounds, then retreats again towards dormancy, providing respite for those of us who surf these dramatic waves. On the farm, we leverage periodic intensifications, seeking to capture as much energy as we can and reinvest it in the soil through matter that will cover, nourish and stitch the ground together.

In the same way we seek to capture finite resources in the shifting expanse of each season. We conserve finite human resources at every point: measuring steps so as not to waste them, aiming always to accomplish several goals in a single trip from the field back to the barn, whether on foot or with petroleum assistance.

We are careful not to waste valuable inputs, whether fertilizer, seed, warm weather or time windows. We avoid activities or negligence that multiply work down the road, protecting our future selves from burdens that would run us aground. On the farm, our steps are calculated, made knowing that energy is valuable, that our time is both sacred and limited. When Jack and I work together, they point out similarities between farm work, ballet and Amazon warehouses, noting that all these involve choreographies following certain rules and forming patterns.

In the parable of the talents, the master berates the land worker who does not invest given resources. Good stewardship is imagined as that which yields returns and minimizes opportunity costs. The lesson seems an assertion of the 'law' of the free market, as under capitalism 'for to everyone who has, more shall be given, and he will have an abundance; but from the one who does not have, even what he does have shall be taken away'.[49] The rich get richer, and the poor get poorer when they don't play by the rules of the game.

While regenerative stewardship and land management play important roles in our fight against extractivism and climate change, there are unintended consequences in solutions that have us employing technical fixes in ways that look remarkably like our problem's cause. The logic we apply to land management and environmental problems defines problems as resource use, and does little to address land sovereignty or histories of land dispossession. So long as we believe land a scarce resource and the products of the land to be limited, we will be tempted to further exclude. For those who conceive of environments as resources, population growth becomes the primary environmental problem. We ignore the imposed economic 'laws' of a system which manufactures scarcity and, instead of sharing land's wealth, we hoard. Here, ecofascism bares its teeth, blaming immigrants and the dispossessed for problems born of the systemic inequities that create both poverty and excessive wealth. With the master's tools, we can unwittingly become the master we'd meant to fight.[50] Speaking of resources risks a colonial move: feeding a culture that presumes access to Indigenous land to benefit settler society.[51] What happens when our attempts to protect land's value preserve the problem and obscure what's at stake?

Terra nullius myths deemed land unoccupied because existing land relations did not fit European, colonial expectations of agricultural productivity. 'Unproductive' land could be reclaimed by those who would steward land resources to maximize benefit for the settler state. *Terra nullius* reifies the modern, European, self-possessed, *homo economicus* farmer, relegating subaltern others to the status of nonhuman while reclaiming their 'wastelands'[52] to advance the 'wise use' of colonial control.[53] It still marginalizes land and people viewed as underproductive, leaving the divide between nature and humans – resources and resource managers – firmly intact, a still-potent tool of dispossession.

Land as verb

But the land *was* never and *is* never empty. It has always been a collection of processes, unfolding in response to the actions and disturbances of many others – of decisions made and desires imported by those who came before. As much as I would like the task of managing this land from which I now live to be uncomplicated, I must reckon continually with its past. My practice and my care must be responsive to its history and memory. Looking carefully, I find clues from which I form hypotheses and plan restorative action. The stories I tell and the actions I test are always evaluated against the land, always changing and revealing new depth in the retelling.

I begin with the most obvious observation: the ground I work is wet, topographically situated near to several waterways that surge with storms. Another clue: this place's namesake, 'Stony Brook', before its now well-known name took hold, a community unto itself, made of farmers, cows and the little waterway now mostly hidden by trees, fences and roads. I notice, talking to neighbour farmers, that my ground is unusually wet, because I can't work the soil when they can. I notice it is always a bit cooler than the weather station predicts, as my plants show signs of frost damage when they shouldn't. I notice, when I slip my trowel into uncultivated ground, that the grass root systems are shallow, and the milky grey colour of this dense silt loam struggling to percolate has little organic matter left from which plant roots and critters might feed. I see, too, iron deposits deep down like crystals, another clue to this place's history: telling me the soil has been saturated enough, for long enough, to develop anaerobic conditions, hydric soils, leaving in the profile traces of an iron redux from beings who had to scavenge and synthesize oxygen in novel ways and from other sources in order to survive here.

I observe discomforts in the land work, too. In the summer season, I find ticks suck at my scalp daily, and while they are mostly dog ticks, this makes my work more stressful. I notice the heat of the summer, of course, the humidity and the way it causes both me and the greens to wilt. I notice flecks of paint in the soil near the barn (lead, likely), and the bits of plastic, a more recent pollutant trucked in with the leaf mulch and compost, the organic matter we need. I notice certain kinds of trash more in an age of pandemic: masks and latex gloves used for our protection from an immediate threat, contributing quietly to a more widespread and pervasive one: plastic pollution, *prolific*.

Land, in the popular imagination, is a thing (noun), but it is also a verb (as in *to land*). We define and map contested borders of land, but land is also a thing one *does*. On the farm, land is what we inherit but also what we *make*, and to farm one must first land (somewhere). Importing compost and plastic, we change soil profiles, as do floodplains and waters, and the migratory and domesticated animals who alike fertilize our fields.

The same applies to many of the processes we use to make land: *compost, manure, soil*. All these are nouns perhaps more accurately thought of (and enacted) as verbs. Compost is, in the end, both product and act, and finished compost is never really finished, but used to inoculate more, later decomposing to again enliven soil. Without the process responsible for its existence and potent to confer ongoing processes of transformation, compost is not compost; its value lies in the quality of the *process* (another verb-noun). *To manure*, too, is to fertilize organically (though this verb has fallen out of fashion): to strategically spread animal (or plant) refuse in ways that feed and regenerate the community that constitutes land in place.[54] Soil – *to soil* – rings dirty in our ears.[55] Its usage reconnects our bodily processes to that of the land – from which we were truly never separate, despite our worst intentions. These land-making acts make other noun-verbs possible: *(to) plant, (to) harvest*. The list could go on.

Land is less static than it is a living entity; it is less being than doing. The doing is what matters (the doing making matter). Our vicar at a church called The Advocate was fond of blurring the strictures of inherited grammars, exhorting our gathered group to 'be the noun, do the verb'.[56] The invitation reminded us that identity and action are inherently linked. It is a repeated pattern: creative animals become fused with their creations, in a state some know as extended cognition.[57] Fungi and tentacular creatures alike spin webs and branch to feel, think and comprehend their environments, as a way to create those environments – the environments that, in turn, create the conditions for their existence.[58] When the strings of its web are pulled or damaged, a spider exhibits psychological stress.[59] They cannot be 'well' apart from the integrity of the environment they create for themselves – the environment that feeds them by digesting and metabolizing the plant and animal lives of this utterly material world.[60]

Humans, too, create environments that metabolize the once-lives of others into arrangements that facilitate the work to feed them. Farms are an obvious example, but cities, too, perform this function, composed of soil-borne and mined elements (brick, steel and sand for concrete) to construct paths along which ever more land-derived resources travel. Through this urban metabolism, consisting of players whose functions are too numerous to count, agricultural products (food, fibre, fuel) become transformed through a series of canals and roads, warehouses, kitchens and dining rooms. All these energy flows derive from living soil, beyond the product on our plate; the plate itself is sourced from soil (whether ceramic or plastic). Air and water move through it. Fire helps carbon return to it. All is soil.

Turns out this land is not empty. Turns out our gods are not dead. The land, still alive despite all the violence and abuse it remembers, is speaking, even *yelling* at us in a language we might still understand. Turns out *terra nullius* was not empty, but merely incomprehensible (*terra incognita*) to the nearsighted mapmaker who sought a god's-eye view.[61]

Terra nullius. A toxic habit of thought, word and deed which worked to make the land empty as it desired. *Terra incognita* transformed through the violence of mapmaking to render the unknown transparent and exploitable. *Terra nullius*, a fiction still working nefariously to terraform us, too ... until we resist, composting and composing words, ourselves and the land otherwise, alongside the agents already making and sustaining the life we barely see.

The work of water: a prayer

I am watching water move across land I thought was flat, pacing, looking down, and paying attention to every detail of this topography. I flood this field using technologies both rudimentary and complex, low-tech but requiring a skill I have not learned. Flood irrigation mimics the disturbance events that made this land, but its frequency adds pressure. Playing God, I try my best to control the water and the way it moves across this deceptively uneven ground, mimicking larger hydrologies. I am haunted by this field when I shut my eyes to sleep, by all I cannot control and all I cannot see.

So many see landownership as a path to freedom. It is less freedom than responsibility, and work. Ownership and work are different kinds of stewardship. A stewardship of ownership concerns itself with value, relying on the labour of others to see value maintained and increased. Those who work land know it costs us our lives.

Settlers saw untamed wilderness, obscuring the labour of those who stewarded these vast and living landscapes, naming, claiming property a resource for empire.

And yet, my soil science teacher tells me it is nearly impossible to kill soil.

Notes

1 Amitav Ghosh describes the 'Europeanization' of the Americas, and the efforts of colonists to create 'Neo-Europes' through imported agricultural practices that terraformed existing agricultural landscapes indiscernible to them. Amitav Ghosh, 2022, *The Nutmeg's Curse: Parables for a Planet in Crisis*, University of Chicago Press; Whitney A. Bauman, 2007, 'Creatio Ex Nihilo, Terra Nullius, and the Erasure of Presence', in Laurel Kearns and Catherine Keller (eds), *Ecospirit: Religions and Philosophies for the Earth*, Fordham University Press, pp. 353–72.

2 Bruno Latour and Peter Weibel, 2020, *Critical Zones: The Science and Politics of Landing on Earth*, MIT Press.

3 Ryan Juskus, 'Sacrifice Zones: A Genealogy and Analysis of an Environmental Justice Concept', *Environmental Humanities*, 15(1) (2023), pp. 3–24, https://doi.org/10.1215/22011919-10216129.

4 Emma Lietz Bilecky, 'The Flood. Deluge', *The Mad Agriculture Journal*, 12 November 2021, https://madagriculture.org/journal/the-flood-deluge, accessed 06.06.2025.

5 Frieda Knobloch, 2000, *The Culture of Wilderness: Agriculture as Colonization in the American West*, University of North Carolina Press.

6 Rupa Marya and Raj Patel, 2021, *Inflamed: Deep Medicine and the Anatomy of Injustice*, Farrar, Straus and Giroux.

7 Tom I. Romero II, 'The Color(Blind) Conundrum in Colorado Property Law', *University of Colorado Law Review*, 94(2) (2023), pp. 449–532.

8 Rebecca Earle, 2014, *The Body of the Conquistador: Food, Race and the Colonial Experience in Spanish America, 1492–1700*, reprint edn, Cambridge University Press.

9 María Puig de la Bellacasa, 'Making Time for Soil: Technoscientific Futurity and the Pace of Care', *Social Studies of Science*, 45(5) (2015), pp. 691–716, https://doi.org/10.1177/0306312715599851.

10 'The idea that the character of different races is shaped, or even determined, by climate has been one of the more enduring in the intellectual history of climate.' Mike Hulme, 2009, 'The Social Meanings of Climate', in *Why We Disagree about Climate Change: Understanding Controversy, Inaction and Opportunity*, Cambridge University Press, p. 19.

11 Clifford R. Lovin, 'Blut und Boden: The Ideological Basis of the Nazi Agricultural Program', *Journal of the History of Ideas*, 28(2) (1967), pp. 279–88, https://doi.org/10.2307/2708423.

12 For matter as *mater* (mother), see J. Kameron Carter, 'Anarchē; or, The Matter of Charles Long and Black Feminism', *American Religion*, 2(2) (2020), pp. 103–35, https://doi.org/10.2979/amerreli.2.2.07.

13 'Rain fulfils its duty as it falls because it was given the gift of sustaining life. What is the duty of humans? If gifts and responsibilities are one,

then asking "What is our responsibility?" is the same as asking "What is our gift?"' Robin Kimmerer, 2013, *Braiding Sweetgrass: Indigenous Wisdom, Scientific Knowledge and the Teachings of Plants*, Milkweed Editions, p. 115.

14 Daniel deB. Richter and Dan H. Yaalon, '"The Changing Model of Soil" Revisited', *Soil Science Society of America Journal*, 76(3) (2012), pp. 766–78, https://doi.org/10.2136/sssaj2011.0407.

15 Richter and Yaalon, '"The Changing Model of Soil" Revisited'.

16 Fairfax Harrison, 'The Crooked Plow', *The Classical Journal*, 11(6) (1916), pp. 323–32.

17 Simon Baatz, 1985, *Venerate the Plow: A History of the Philadelphia Society for Promoting Agriculture 1785–1985*, Philadelphia Society for Promoting Agriculture.

18 In the West, agriculturalists falsely believed 'the rain [would follow] the plow'. See Marc Reisner, 1993, *Cadillac Desert: The American West and Its Disappearing Water*, revised edn, Penguin.

19 Nicole Masters, 2019, *For the Love of Soil: Strategies to Regenerate Our Food Production Systems*, Integrity Soils Limited.

20 'The plowshare may well have destroyed more options for future generations than the sword.' Wes Jackson, 1980, *New Roots for Agriculture*, University of Nebraska Press, p. 2.

21 Levi Van Sant, '"The Long-Time Requirements of the Nation": The US Cooperative Soil Survey and the Political Ecologies of Improvement', *Antipode*, 53(3) (2021), pp. 686–704, https://doi.org/10.1111/anti.12460.

22 Knobloch, *The Culture of Wilderness*.

23 David A. Wardle, 1999, 'How Soil Food Webs Make Plants Grow', *Trends in Ecology & Evolution*, 14(11) (1999), pp. 418–20, https://doi.org/10.1016/S0169-5347(99)01640-7.

24 David R. Montgomery, 2017, *Growing a Revolution: Bringing Our Soil Back to Life*, W. W. Norton & Company.

25 This story was given to me by Nancy, who grew up on the farmland of the Farminary that this story references.

26 William Langland, 1996, *Piers Plowman: The C Version*, trans. George Economou, University of Pennsylvania Press.

27 Sarah Augustine, 2021, *The Land Is Not Empty: Following Jesus in Dismantling the Doctrine of Discovery*, Herald Press, p. 27.

28 William Cronon, 2003, *Changes in the Land: Indians, Colonists, and the Ecology of New England*, Hill and Wang, a division of Farrar, Straus and Giroux (first published 1983).

29 John Locke, 1821, *Two Treatises of Government*, Whitmore and Fenn, pp. 208–30.

30 Bauman, 'Creatio Ex Nihilo'.

31 Kimmerer, *Braiding Sweetgrass*, p. 208.

32 Ruth A. Meyers and Leonel L. Mitchell, 2016, *Praying Shapes*

Believing: A Theological Commentary on the Book of Common Prayer, revised edn, Church Publishing, Inc.

33 'Prayers for National Life'.

34 Betsy Gaines Quammen, 2020, *American Zion: Cliven Bundy, God & Public Lands in the West*, Torrey House Press.

35 J. Michael Hunter, 'The Desert Shall Blossom as the Rose: Pioneering Irrigation / John A. Widtsoe', *Pioneer* (Summer 2003), pp. 10–14, 24–25.

36 Ghosh, *The Nutmeg's Curse*, p. 49.

37 Ghosh, *The Nutmeg's Curse*, p. 49.

38 See Lauret Savoy, 2015, *Trace: Memory, History, Race, and the American Landscape*, Catapult.

39 See Robin Kimmerer, 2013, 'The Sacred and the Superfund', in *Braiding Sweetgrass*, pp. 310–40.

40 Carol M. Rose, 2019, *Property and Persuasion: Essays on the History, Theory, and Rhetoric of Ownership*, Routledge. See also Cheryl I. Harris, 'Whiteness as Property', *Harvard Law Review*, 106(8) (1993), pp. 1707–91, https://doi.org/10.2307/1341787.

41 Madeleine Fairbairn, 2020, *Fields of Gold: Financing the Global Land Rush*, Cornell University Press.

42 Madeleine Fairbairn writes that farmland is frequently referred to as 'black gold', as 'like gold with yield' or as 'gold with a coupon'. Madeleine Fairbairn, '"Like Gold with Yield": Evolving Intersections between Farmland and Finance', *The Journal of Peasant Studies*, 41(5) (2014), pp. 777–95, p. 785.

43 Connor Ryan and Tim Kressin (dirs), *Spirit of the Peaks*, 2021, https://www.rei.com/blog/spirit-of-the-peaks-film, accessed 15.07.2023.

44 See, for example, Dana E. Powell, 2018, *Landscapes of Power: Politics of Energy in the Navajo Nation*, Duke University Press, 2018. Also recall the fight over Bears Ears National Monument under the first Trump administration.

45 Paula DiPerna, 2023, *Pricing the Priceless: The Financial Transformation to Value the Planet, Solve the Climate Crisis, and Protect Our Most Precious Assets*, Wiley. See also Aldo Leopold, 2020, 'Land Health and the A-B Cleavage', in *A Sand County Almanac: And Sketches Here and There*, Oxford University Press, pp. 208–9, and Elizabeth Kolbert, 2021, *Under a White Sky: The Nature of the Future*, Crown.

46 Garrett Hardin, 'The Tragedy of the Commons', *Science*, 162(3859) (1968), pp. 1243–48, https://doi.org/10.1126/science.162.3859.1243; Elinor Ostrom, Joanna Burger, Christopher B. Field, Richard B. Norgaard and David Policansky, 'Revisiting the Commons: Local Lessons, Global Challenges', *Science*, 284(5412) (1999), pp. 278–82, https://doi.org/10.1126/science.284.5412.278; Elinor Ostrom, 2015, *Governing the Commons*, Cambridge University Press; Andrew P. Follett, Brigham Daniels, and Taylor Petersen, 2021, 'The Tragedy of Garrett Hardin's

Commons', in Chrystie F. Swiney and Sheila R. Foster, *The Cambridge Handbook of Commons Research Innovations*, Cambridge University Press, pp. 26–33.

47 Lynn White, 'The Historical Roots of Our Ecologic Crisis', *Science*, 155(3767) (1967), pp. 1203–7, https://doi.org/10.1126/science.155.3767.1203.

48 Brian D. McLaren, 2024, *Life after Doom: Wisdom and Courage for a World Falling Apart*, St. Martin's Publishing Group.

49 Matthew 25.29.

50 Audre Lorde, 2018, *The Master's Tools Will Never Dismantle the Master's House*, Penguin Books Limited.

51 Max Liboiron describes colonialism as presumed access to Indigenous land for settler purposes. Max Liboiron, 2021, *Pollution Is Colonialism*, Duke University Press.

52 Traci Brynne Voyles, 2015, *Wastelanding: Legacies of Uranium Mining in Navajo Country*, University of Minnesota Press.

53 Calum Murray, 'John Locke's Theory of Property, and the Dispossession of Indigenous Peoples in the Settler-Colony', *American Indian Law Journal*, 10 (2022), pp. 55–67.

54 Saskia Cornes, 'Milton's Manuring: *Paradise Lost*, Husbandry, and the Possibilities of Waste', *Milton Studies*, 61(1) (March 1, 2019), pp. 65–85, https://doi.org/10.5325/miltonstudies.61.1.0065.

55 David R. Montgomery, 2007, *Dirt: The Erosion of Civilizations*, University of California Press.

56 Lisa G. Fischbeck, 2021, *Behold What You Are: Becoming the Body of Christ*, Church Publishing, Incorporated.

57 Sophie Strand, 'On Happiness: Becoming Ecologically Embedded with Sophie Strand', *Sleek*, 11 January 2023, https://www.sleek-mag.com/article/on-happiness-becoming-ecologically-embedded-with-sophie-strand/.

58 Strand, 'On Happiness'.

59 Hilton F. Japyassú and Kevin N. Laland, 'Extended Spider Cognition', *Animal Cognition*, 20(3) (2017), pp. 375–95, https://doi.org/10.1007/s10071-017-1069-7.

60 Merlin Sheldrake, 2020, *Entangled Life: How Fungi Make Our Worlds, Change Our Minds and Shape Our Futures*, Penguin Random House.

61 Kei Miller, 2014, *The Cartographer Tries to Map a Way to Zion*, Carcanet Press Limited.

3

Compost Cosmologies

Summer solstice

Summer solstice arrives unexpectedly. Days lengthen to match quickening pace, and to-do lists still exceed available light. By this time of year, most of the planting is behind us. It is too late to change many plans. Still, the work is ahead. We have organized and facilitated the growth we now hand off to the soil, to the unexpected elements and circumstances beyond our control. We continue to cultivate, and we look towards larger harvests. And yet it is in the midst of this activity that the first signs of winter appear. A solstice is a turning point from steady expansion towards imperceptible contraction. A descent into darkness from this peak begins early, even before the worst heat comes. This season holds together life just beginning with death foreshadowed. The liveliest, hottest and hardest of days are balanced by darkness underneath and ahead.

Everything is compost

We are standing around the compost pile, its smell wafting on the hot breath of the air to meet our noses. This pile is leaky and smells anaerobic, reflecting back to us that we are still learning, still perfecting the recipe, not yet fully trained or attuned to the many dynamics at work here. 'There are good ways and worse ways of composting,' I tell the small crowd gathered. Compost itself, you see, is ubiquitous.

There are many kinds of compost processes at work on this farm. Some work better and more quickly than others. The big compost pile is obvious from the entrance: a long windrow whose heat releases steam in the first hours of morning light. We combine into piles what is available regionally and seasonally. For us, that's food waste from nearby student housing, and leaves from our deciduous ornamentals that otherwise clog gutters and roads. If we are paying attention, we monitor the windrow's moisture and temperature to achieve the right balance of more and less recently dead plant matter. We call these components 'greens' or 'browns' according to their nitrogen content.

But we are not the only composters rearranging available matter to meet our needs. Leaves on the forest floor make compost – leaf mould – as do hens scratching and fertilizing the soil, as do mycelia weaving their ways by digesting downed tree limbs. Composting is happening all around us, performed by many to achieve many outcomes. The goal is to facilitate the kinds of compost we want.

I remember my grandmother explaining to me how her family made compost on their Iowa farm. While the process served dual purposes of reducing waste and recycling nutrients, 'compost' had no such designation. Plant matter from the garden and the field, sometimes mixed with manure, broke down to feed soil. Compost happened, daily and continually, but it was so unremarkable it went unnamed.

Before the plastics industry invented trash[1] – first a novel concept, and, soon after, a choking, ever-present reality – compost was the stuff of life, and the stuff of life was compost. Without its foil – that trash that could not in the same way become ground again within the bounds of human timescales – compost was nothing exceptional. If matter is neither created nor destroyed, and carbon constantly cycles through complex exchanges between ground and atmosphere within this thin skin of the earth where everything happens,[2] isn't everything organic matter?

If you've ever asked what happens to compostables buried in plastic deep underground in anaerobic environments, I might answer: something similar to what happens to a chemically laden, embalmed body, sealed in a coffin – not much, not very quickly, at least. But, though they interrupt and delay the return, even plastics transmuted from oil made of dinosaur bodies derive from a living, breathing source.

Nowadays, when buried trash causes land's indigestion, compost has become special, imbued with salvific powers. What farmers call compost today names a faster return to soil. The compost pile accelerates organic matter's breakdown in ways that foster life – the right combination of elements in the right place at the right time, teeming with microbes. Leaf litter decomposing on streets and drained into waterways cannot do the same, deeply transformative work in an endless sea of concrete – the proportions of elements are not quite right for transformation. But compost, added strategically to depleted soil at the right time and in the right way, is the basis of fertility.

Good compost is a matter of proportions. Like a recipe, compost happens when the specific ingredients are present and combined in a specific way. Chemically speaking, compost does well in the presence of oxygen (although there are some exceptions) and water when the ratio of carbon to nitrogen (by weight) is about 30 to 1. On our farm, it looks like this: food scraps collected are sandwiched between thicker layers of leaf mulch collected in the fall and inoculated with finished compost, full of the life we want. Compost piles are turned every few days to infuse them with oxygen, invigorating the microbes and energizing them to break down others and generate the heat needed to neutralize risky pathogens.

But it also happens like this: a pile of leaves, sitting for many years, steaming sometimes. Even untouched by human hands, this compost is always at work. This compost is like gold, Chucho, our compost consultant and guide, says. These microbes work like God: invisible, omnipotent, making new life. Chucho is helping us see these ceaseless but subtle processes, this work of the world so easy to miss. He is digging in our compost pile, enthusiastically, finding green growth emergent from buried corn cobs. He inhales deeply, sensing microscopic communion and collaboration with his nose. He tells us the small ones are everywhere. He talks to them and shows us how to find them.

We are harvesting bacteria from the land, from the compost, from forest soil whose webs of life are intact and communicative

– more so than the disturbed soil of our cultivated land. This compost process is *fermentative*, capturing the kinds of microbes who make alcohol, who can speed and aid the processes by which bones, meat and animal parts are digested. They counteract the growth of pathogens and make better compost – compost that does not release methane. To grow these indigenous microbial populations, we create environments for their thriving and reproduction with water sweetened with mineral-rich molasses, causing microbes harvested from this corn cob to feed and to multiply.

Though we tend to think soil a 'thing', the earth and its soils contain multitudes beyond our comprehension and beyond our naming,[3] always eating and making food for many we cannot see in the largely invisible 'soil food web'.[4] Small ones sustain life across trophic levels; their ability to sustain our living and growing food is but a byproduct of their function. A landscape is a foodscape, a boisterous buffet.

As soil's relationality – eating and being eaten – is interrupted through the disturbance of earth-moving, building or chemicals, soil's liveliness is degraded. Too often, we readily rid ourselves of the small ones we need – insects and microbes in our soils, doused in glyphosate, or in our homes baptized with Lysol – even as we profess our dependence on a world divinely designed and ordained. We praise the artist and architect while destroying that which is their creation and, at the same time, the very possibility of ours.

The microbiomes of land and bodies touch and shape us intimately. Our internal microbial worlds suffer from declining diversity in step with degraded soils, devoid of the life that sustains them after repeated attacks.[5] The trends between the two run parallel, and are perhaps linked, as the declining biodiversity of soils accompanies the declining nutritional quality of the food that feeds us and our intestinal worlds in turn.

This age of acceleration is also one of annihilation. As our climate changes, it is increasingly a climate of death, one in which a great number of us cannot survive within the places and temperature ranges in which we evolved. We are in the midst of a sixth great extinction,[6] with an incomprehensible number of life forms being lost forever – much faster than in the past, and much faster than they can adapt to new environments. And yet we may not perceive all this dying around us, perhaps because we do not know or notice the animals around us, or perhaps because they are too small, or perhaps because we have no language with which to mourn what's going on.[7] While we mourn the white rhinoceros and other charismatic megafauna, we may forget the threatened insects and their essential but invisible labour, pollinating and decomposing the world. Still, I wonder: can the mycelia, soil fungi and bacteria we grow break down what is toxic in our soils? Is it just to ask these small ones to break down the toxins we have not stopped releasing into their environments? What will breakdown look like in hotter, dryer places, where the scarcity of water limits or slows bacterial or fungal growth? What responsibility do we have to those we ask to repair what we have harmed?[8]

As farmers and hobbyists have rediscovered the power of compost to reanimate tired soils in ways more enduring than the synthetic chemicals that promised cheap, fast and magical solutions, many have also found compost to contain power beyond its measure. Compost shows us ways forward that break binaries intent on the bifurcation of life and death, the living and the dead, forward and backward movement. Compost testifies that growth yields decay, and decay, growth. That death follows life, and life, death. Compost tells stories of transformation and transforms old stories. Some see in compost a site for mourning. The processual transformations that both compost and grief accomplish can be messy and painful. In the middle of compost, we may not see what's going on. Compost takes time to cure, as grief needs time to be metabolized before its work is done.

Compost offers us a way to think about loss in an age of too-many, too-soon deaths, a measure of hope that the losses we grieve will yet yield something: that *loss is also a beginning*. But if compost is to symbolize for us some kind of hope in and through the tragedies we witness and those we feel, its symbolic power is ultimately grounded in the activity itself. Compost is not merely what happens, but what we do. Compost is both noun and verb.

Land work

There are many ways to tend a garden, to hold in balance the countless objectives, directions and lives that together constitute this living system. Those who quietly pay attention to the ever-shifting dynamics at play can discern these overlapping trajectories and notice the ways the land's past shapes the land's present. Even absent a caretaker-guide, a garden speaks to those skilled to listen. The decisions and desires of many are inscribed on the land, even seasons after they are made. The land responds slowly to decisions made in an instant; it absorbs and remembers the impacts we too soon forget.

Because this half-acre was too large for us to manage, we turned half the space into an eventually unruly series of compost piles. The compost-fallow was a way to emulate adherence to that Levitical directive to let the land rest. But what we learned from this experiment is that the land has no pause button – the soil never sleeps.[9] At best, winter's metabolic slowdown provides the farmer with reprieve, but the many lives of soil and compost keep moving, if slowly. When reawakened in the height and heat of summer, the soil and the decomposers who feed it continue *their* agricultural production – germinating seeds we did not see or anticipate.

In our attempts to enforce rest in the wrong season, we sought permission to ignore a part of the garden continuing to work despite the absence of ours. What proliferated was not only weeds but the multiplication of work required in response. A compost pile left alone grows weeds strong and powerful. And even after their individual lives wane in winter, the seed they leave dormant in this now more fertile soil are poised to emerge before the plants and seeds we choose, forever after.

Years after a decision to leave this portion of the garden 'fallow', we are still battling weeds whose seeds first took root without our interference. The weed seed bank grows plants suited to disturbed soils that also provide certain benefits. Purslane (pigweed) is prolific but edible, crunchy and tangy. Mugwort with it root runners is medicine, used for insomnia and dreams. Jimsonweed is terribly prickly, but conceals in its massive seed pods psychoactive compounds. These are not the plants whose growth supports our farm financially, as they are not the plants that members of our community-supported agricultural programme or local restaurants seek. So these get called weeds, though they are in many ways beneficial and uniquely able to tell us about the state of our soil. When named weeds, they become problems in the heavily managed, cultivated market farm space whose margins are often too slim for this level of chaos.

Some say agriculture is our human vocation. The soil is imprinted in ways we know and call ourselves – humans, of humus. They say agriculture is what sets us apart from supposedly less intelligent creatures, who find rather than create food-bearing landscapes. Through agriculture human creatures re-engineer landscapes and water cycles, making liveable desolate places and taming wild ones.

In agriculture, the earth we seek to subdue with our heavy machines is lively for reasons we haven't always understood – its liveliness has been viewed as a barrier to be overcome instead. In soil communities left alone, the soil surface is always covered, never bare. Walk through the woods and you'll see every inch of ground covered with leaf litter: pine needles, rotting tree trunks and mushrooms marking mycelial life underground. Green growth emerges out of this patchy ground, as plants form pathways and partnerships alongside plants of other kinds with other growing habits. Some provide shade, while some spread to cover the ground, while still others look upward for light.

By contrast, much of agriculture begins with the destruction of ecological diversity. Disc harrows pulverize interconnected root systems to make way for new seeds brought in from elsewhere. Seedbed preparation begins by clearing the plant debris that shades and nourishes soil life and pulling apart the mycorrhizal threads that serve as soil's embedded communication network. Seeds planted grow alongside one another in neat and tidy rows, spaced carefully to provide optimal space, light, moisture and root zone for plants of the same variety. New seeds compete with those dormant in 'stale' soil; the farmer may aid their fight with chemicals or cultivation. All this mechanical and chemical interference yields results novel in nature – vast areas of little biodiversity. In this schema, the farmer fights the natural inclinations of the soil, making instead a universe of humans' design, out of sync with the patterns and processes that made the soil fertile in the first place.

There is no way to know how many seeds still lie dormant in the soil, but for now and into the near future, they emerge in droves every spring. We cannot change our situation, but we can respond to an unchangeable past, looking towards our shared future with ever more limited possibilities. Where bad decisions have multiplied work, now, by the sweat of our brow, we continue. We do not abandon our duty to care for degraded soil merely because we resent the necessity to repair past harm. This is no reason to give up.

Being compost

Compost, as I understand it, is a community and an environment at once. Compost is a microcosmic terrapolis[10] that takes shape and structure by the traces its microscopic members leave and the webs they weave. Compost is a vital medium for restoring soils, contributing organic matter to the soil food web, but not yet soil itself.[11] Compost is the partially decomposed bodies of animals and plants which grow from it, a medium that brings forth life at the same time that it is itself a living collectivity.

Compost is not one thing but many beings, who share an environment while feasting on the environment they create. In this heap, organic matter feeds bacteria, feeding protozoa or fungi, who feed nematodes, then arthropods, then animals. There is a temptation to read into compost, wherein larger beings consume smaller ones across trophic levels, a kind of carnage, a food chain where unfriendly competitors feast upon one another's decay. But though eating always involves death, not all eating is deadly. This is not a game with winners and losers. And while the act of feeding entails the cessation of some individuality, it also, at the very same time, creates the conditions for each life's emergence. No *one* can exist separated from the whole. As Donna Haraway says, 'we become with each other, or not at all'.[12]

Lest we be tempted to extract ourselves from this mess, to deduce from a distance a dispassionate meaning from it, consider: where are you in the compost pile? More than an instrumental medium or a singular *thing*, compost is an environment we together create. People are as much a part of it as anyone else. 'We are walking compost,' says Aimé Césaire, preserved from the death we daily digest only for a little while.[13] We compose and decompose this compost, together with the springtails. Contributions of our manure and our atrophying muscle power feed the pile in the same way those decomposing plant bodies do, and while we may guide the pile in a particular direction according to our desires and our tastes, our will does not singularly determine the way this compost goes – we attend to the needs and desires of many others, too.

Compost may be happening all around us, but, in an age of rapid soil erosion, desertification and violent terraformations, machinations, compaction and the suppression of soil life, we'd do best to speed up this process, so long as we hope to live in fertile places and feast on nutrient-dense foods. Our senses show us, too, what kinds of compost we desire. That smell that turns up noses indicates a compost heap that, far from sequestering atmospheric carbon, is releasing methane, a more potent greenhouse gas. The moisture level of healthy compost, like a wet sponge, should invite our touch, not repel it. Our senses, attuned to the complex dynamics and divergent desires of this more-than-human muddle[14] can show us the way, if we're paying attention. We learn by doing, responding to this environment perpetually in flux. Our belief in the power of life is tested and refined here – and is only as powerful as our practice. We observe, we respond, we tinker,[15] and we find a way, even as we find our action is always limited by that of others. There are good and worse ways of making compost, ways that make the life we want more or less possible.

In compost, we don't just consume resources but, together with innumerable others, we produce what we need. Rather than extracting resources from the earth through technologically assisted violence, compost is a way we return what we take. It is the inverse of mining, which extracts value while deteriorating its source leaving tailing piles that continue to pollute long after.[16]

The dominant economy conceives resource extraction as a one-way street. A long and complex supply chain connects a point of extraction, remote, intensive and concealed from the view of too many, to a point of consumption, distributed and devoid of geography. The energy wired into homes consolidates vast and varied energy supply chains, but to the one who consumes or conserves commodified electricity, the energy that animates a lightbulb neither retains nor evokes the memory of its earthly source. The electricity that illuminates our dwellings, like building materials that coalesce to create shelter, like food that not only fuels but also becomes our bodies, comes to us through people and from places, though manufactured not to reveal either. This is a theological problem.

Instead of adapting to changing landscapes, we adapt our lives to untrue economic maxims, out of sync with the ecologies from which they derive. Dominant economic theories are based on ecological fallacies: endless growth, discounted futures, a consumer who is never consumed. Daily, we impose a false linearity on cyclical processes, thinking more of output, productivity and accumulation than the loss and decay that are their necessary counterparts. Every day our consumption returns waste, whether manure or mine tailings. All along we are becoming compost. In this we have no choice, though we may still together decide *how* – whether our lives will produce waste that burdens the landscapes that feed us[17] or food that nourishes the landscapes we become.

The story of agriculture in the United States is a story of progress. The progress we praise was mined from the soil. Land's perpetual improvement through agriculture has always sought as its end increased extraction from soil. Agricultural improvements seek to maximize productivity so that higher yields feed growing populations. Under the pressures of productivity we've drained wetlands and flooded deserts, destroyed soil structure with the power of the plow, and reworked biodiverse landscapes and foodscapes to produce ever more of the commodified staples of European diets in a kind of culinary colonization, regardless of the regional variation of the lands from which they derive.[18]

All these stories proceed on linear timelines, beginning, unfolding and concluding along a unidirectional arc. Even the stories we tell of civilization's imminent demise satisfy the urge to conclude – to see to the end, and no further. Apocalypse is appealing, for it does not ask us to see another way besides the worst. The real and imagined catastrophes of climate change satisfy desires for linear storylines. Even if terrifying, these grand, apocalyptic conclusions – that the world will end the way we fear – comfort us for their familiarity. Christian stories encode a death drive in progress narratives, craving the assurance of prophecy, even as it accelerates many deaths and extinctions.

Compost may make land more productive, but it resists historicization. Compost has no ending; even once finished, its purpose is ongoing. Generations do not build upon one another so much as they feed on each other's refuse instead. Compost stories remake linear models and fixed property lines with a longer and deeper view from which we can see earth's curvature. Compost reshapes the flat earths where many of us still live.

Compost, surely, has a use, but its end is not static. To *be* compost is *to* compost: the name implies activity. Compost is process: digested, digestion and digesting. A stable medium, momentarily, but ultimately soil's food. And, just like food, compost's transformation is potent to transform: to imbibe soil with organic matter, soil movers pull down soil profiles.

Compost seeks balance, in process and in application. Too much compost can cause problems of its own in the form of eutrophication downstream, or make nutrients inaccessible to the plants the farmer strives to grow. Once piled up, compost must also be broken down. Its usefulness is proportionate to those lives who would consume it, at the same time as it creates the conditions, therefore making possible new and more life in the place it lands.

I must admit, for all my love of compost, I am uncomfortable with some of its implications. Contemplating new life from death in the compost pile, I am tempted to extract a simple moral from its ongoing story by means of some biological determinism in which dangerous pathologies are overcome by an inevitable redemptive arc. When compost is a metaphor for salvation, it overlooks the importance of our contributions and keeps an individualistic storyline intact. When salvation is figured as purification or ascension, we've already left the muddle. Compost shows that we are not *on* earth as much as we are *in* it, and at every point constituted by it. Compost feeds on us, too. The salvation preached at the table is an ecological reality: we become what we receive.[19]

What separates humans from the other animals?

I seek no such distinction.
To be human – in the *image* of God:
The *ego* of God
self-destructive
all-knowing, deadly power of God
(crafted in the image of the human)
extinguishing species and cultures in all its glory.

Animals are in the love of God
the love that we ate in the garden
before the first humans
all us, animals –
before we grew
we tasted God
we loved them back.

Death is not a metaphor

Natural processes often become metaphors for spiritual realities.[20] Compost is no different. The death that is an integral part of decomposition becomes a teaching tool to help process – and justify – the suffering we experience as part of God's redemptive plan. God can take the most infertile and rocky of soils, so the story goes, and transform them into soils full of life and richness, but we must pass through death to get there: as soil fertility owes itself to countless *things* that have died to become compost-food for the collective good.

I am troubled by this way of narrating soil's life, for there is danger in reifying death through it. It strikes me that this death is out of touch with death as experienced by those who mourn and grieve the loss of a loved one, death that is premature, death by suicide, death that is not redemptive and should not be said to be – death by suffocation and state violence which is unjust and terrible all the way down. The 'death' of ambition is different; our suffering is uneven. The suffering of a friend dead by suicide does not lend itself to easy narration. It sticks. It will not be overcome.

Death is woven into the fabric of this universe, this planet and its evolutionary processes. I am careful, however, not to yield to a social Darwinism that glorifies the loss of the losers for the sake of the (s)elect. Death is with us, eternally, not as a tally or a head count but as the common fate of sinners and saints whose bodies are thoroughly material. It is *our* bodies, their fluid and their bile, which will ultimately become soil's food. There is not much that is flowery or romantic about this.

The ubiquity of death reaches out to touch us. Death is the immense pain of living, a thick worldless memory held in the land. Of course, its ubiquity does not ease its pain, but brings it ever closer. A world of death is a world inhabited by ghosts and saints, an animate world that watches and holds its children. A world that demands everything (your life) but also gives everything (its life) – there is no leaving behind this resurrecting reincarnation. We become the place we are.

The problem is unrecognizing. The task is recognition. To particularize earthy engagements, to see soil biota not as *things* – assets or ecosystem services to be captured in service to soil carbon sequestration *or* theological education – but as lives responsible to their own ends. Or, rather, they are responsible to the ends determined by soil communities through cooperation and symbiosis. Though this gets interpreted as a kind of competition (we go to great lengths to prop up pre-existing ideologies), in reality it is a practice of mutual, collective consent.

As we were working in the garden the other day, weeding, some students were wondering about the personhood of plants, and how to reconcile the decisions we make in cultivation to selectively take lives. Do plants resent the hands of the weeder, we wondered, crying out when individually uprooted? Or is this way of seeing plant life – as responsible only to their own visibly distinct flourishing and thereby ruled by competition – itself a capitalist imposition? Do plants become compost only reluctantly?

It strikes me that the plant wisdom we seek to learn is in large part perspective: a perspective on the workings of processes in which we are a constitutive part but only very minimally in control. Like riding a bike, our presence and our leaning make a difference in the way things go, but our agency is limited by many other forces with which we'd do best to cooperate. As in fermentation, our hand contributes only minimally to the making and rearranging of environments in which other lives flourish and multiply: it is the invisible heterogeneous collective that does the always open-ended work.

Is the gardener's role a kind of chaplaincy, seeking to create conditions for honourable death in good faith? To recognize the particularity of lives and suffering and to seek repair in deep time, through care? Like a chaplain, the care we give is limited by many circumstances we cannot transform. The best we can do is to better live (and die) with them. And not towards some other, spiritual or immaterial end, but as a practice that values – and multiplies the value of – the here, the now, the divine life we continue to share.

To begin in this direction requires recognizing the lives we take and on which we depend. For this reason, responsible theological thinking with soil requires some basic familiarity with soil processes – learning to perceive creatures by name and the traces of their lives and labour. Without attentiveness and care, soil spiritualizations partake in familiar forms of capture: enlisting soil labours in life support for a dying church. Thinking with soil, caring for soil, being transformed with soil, requires knowing soils in the particular, not merely through metaphor. For love is not a metaphor but an active verb (as are compost, soil and manure). How can we love what we do not know? How can we know what we do not touch?

Disintegration, decomposition: a prayer

The land is my limit: showing me where a day's work ends, how much is enough. Not all work has such physical limits. Every day is like this, an arc of ambitions that ends with fatigue. We are gathered up again every evening; the following day, we give it all again. Each day the sun moves through me, its energy never mine to hold on to. The work comes in waves, moving in, receding back, so unlike those progress narratives that pushed me in a singular, forward and upward direction.

Compost is everywhere a reminder of this, a kind of organized entropy, or breakdown. Intact individuals break down to yield intact, alive ecosystems. When the relationship between production and its waste products is severed from land, pollution results.

I see compost all around me: matter in motion with water and atmosphere, in sinking houses with cracking foundations. Water vapour, beading on my skin, also moulds siding. I see matter in motion, never stable. Sitting still enough long enough, homes and streets decompose before my eyes. Land transformed into a stable investment called real estate begins to look a lot different, less stable, more momentary.

Compost happens all around me. All matter on earth contains carbon, eating time and giving it back. What is green in time turns brown, its carbon and nitrogen always in motion between soil and atmosphere.

Notes

1 Laura Sullivan, 'How Big Oil Misled the Public into Believing Plastic Would Be Recycled', *NPR*, Investigations, 11 September 2020, https://www.npr.org/2020/09/11/897692090/how-big-oil-misled-the-public-into-believing-plastic-would-be-recycled, accessed 06.06.2025.

2 Bruno Latour and Peter Weibel, 2020, *Critical Zones: The Science and Politics of Landing on Earth*, MIT Press.

3 Ed Yong, 2016, *I Contain Multitudes: The Microbes Within Us and a Grander View of Life*, Ecco.

4 Jeff Lowenfels and Wayne Lewis, 2014, *Teaming with Microbes: The Organic Gardener's Guide to the Soil Food Web*, Hachette+ORM.

5 David R. Montgomery and Anne Biklé, 2015, *The Hidden Half*

of Nature: The Microbial Roots of Life and Health, W. W. Norton & Company, 2015.

6 Elizabeth Kolbert, 2015, *The Sixth Extinction: An Unnatural History*, Picador.

7 Camille T. Dungy, 'Losing Language', *Emergence Magazine*, 25 June 2019, https://emergencemagazine.org/essay/losing-language/, accessed 06.06.2025.

8 Anna Krzywoszynska, 'Nonhuman Labor and the Making of Resources', *Environmental Humanities*, 12(1) (2020), pp. 227–49, https://doi.org/10.1215/22011919-8142319.

9 Adam Horovitz, 2019, *The Soil Never Sleeps: Poetry from Six British Pasture Farms*, Palewell Press.

10 Donna J. Haraway, 2016, *Staying with the Trouble: Making Kin in the Chthulucene*, Duke University Press.

11 María Puig de la Bellacasa, discussing the work of Elaine Ingham, in 'Making Time for Soil: Technoscientific Futurity and the Pace of Care', *Social Studies of Science*, 45(5) (2015), pp. 691–716, p. 704.

12 Haraway, *Staying with the Trouble*, p. 4.

13 Aimé Césaire, 2001, *Notebook of a Return to the Native Land*, ed. and trans. Clayton Eshleman and Annette Smith, Wesleyan University Press, p. 28.

14 Haraway, *Staying with the Trouble*.

15 Sebastian Abrahamsson and Filippo Bertoni. 'Compost Politics: Experimenting with Togetherness in Vermicomposting', *Environmental Humanities* 4(1) (2014), pp. 125–48.

16 Anna Lowenhaupt Tsing, 2014, 'Blasted Landscapes (and the Gentle Arts of Mushroom Picking)', in Eben Kirksey (ed.), *The Multispecies Salon*, Duke University Press, pp. 87–109.

17 Robin Kimmerer describes the conversion of land to waste in Robin Kimmerer, 2013, 'The Sacred and the Superfund' in *Braiding Sweetgrass: Indigenous Wisdom, Scientific Knowledge and the Teachings of Plants*, Milkweed Editions, pp. 310–40.

18 Sean Sherman contrasts diverse Indigenous foodways with the colonial staples of American diets and their ecological effects. See Sean Sherman, 2017, *The Sioux Chef's Indigenous Kitchen*, University of Minnesota Press.

19 Augustine, 'Sermon 227: Preached on the Holy Day of Easter to the Infantes, on the Sacraments', 414.

20 This section is adapted from Emma Lietz Bilecky, 2022, 'Soil Is Not a Metaphor', *EcoTheo*, https://www.ecotheo.org/etreview/soil-is-not-a-metaphor, accessed 26.06.2025.

4

The Geography of Sin

Midsummer

The middle of summer is the hardest time to farm. It is hot and exhausting, and we are caked constantly in dirt. The diseases and bugs come quickly, spread and multiply, and we attempt to respond to the successive and concurrent pressures we are too late to prevent with too-blunt tools – kaolin clay, Bacillus thuringiensis, Nolo Bait *– that always work better before the problem is this severe. We squish potato beetles and harlequin bugs between dirty fingers, last-resort and time-consuming methods through which we hope to save only so many plants. All this makes me uneasy. We play God but we are bad actors, deciding who lives and who dies, knocking beetles from potato leaves into buckets of soapy water, and allowing weeds to bear seeds when we are too tired to go on. Food is abundant, but we now know too well we are not in control of the innumerable lives – planned and unplanned– that insist on sharing this cultivated space.*

Not only is this work at this time of year unglamorous, muddying images of bucolic farm life, it also attacks our aspirational Edens, troubling our commitment to the cooperative and collaborative principles in which we want to believe on organic farms. Life and death on the farm are often unredemptive, compromised and compromising the ethics and values we struggle to pragmatically uphold, even as we find and feel ourselves swimming upstream against currents we cannot control but only navigate.

We are burdened with responsibility for decisions of recent history – whether our own or those of others – poor planning, earlier shortcuts, overambitious crop plans. Uncontrollable chaos abounds. There is so much to eat, but so little time to sit still. We are immersed in the work as first responders facing successive emergencies and ongoing catastrophes.

The farm is a series of layered and interlocking systems. We are part of these systems, we organize and set some of them in motion, but we do not control their unfolding. Once they begin to function or fail, our options for interference are limited. To correct or modify the course of a living system, we need strategy and we need leverage, for we cannot fight the inertia of a living system with brute force, or alone. We work with and against the amplifying impact of time. Just as small, past actions led to consequences we face today, our wise or alternately heedless minute interferences today will bear impacts far into the future. The trouble is, time doesn't stop.

The heat of midsummer intensifies each year. More than the physical discomfort this intensifying heat brings, there is a pervasive, foreboding anxiety that ruptures in normality relentlessly cause. This experience is not merely our own. We are part of something larger and we know it. Whether we witness our own catastrophe or are spared this year, each year, we calculate the risks ahead. Every summer we see chaos unfold on farms like ours. Farmers spread mud on tunnel plastic to deflect sunlight amid heat domes. Farmers wait through prolonged droughts for rare gifts of rain, doing what they can to help the soil conserve scarce water when seasonal monsoons fail to arrive as they have so predictably from time immemorial, now disrupted and rearranged. Each season, we carry the weight of each other's loss. It reminds us of our shared and growing precarity.

Farming in the summer as global temperatures rise, we feel ourselves part of nested systems – climate systems, social systems and ecological systems – we hardly control. A farm is a microcosm within a microclimate and with microclimates of its own. In a system whose complexity multiplies endlessly, farmers learn where our intervention makes impact, if we can pay attention.

Bad faith

It is difficult to hold one's gaze. It takes practice to pay attention. Climate breakdown looms large, and lurks in the recesses of our collective unconscious. Though we seek to render this change invisible and impotent by turning our backs on the warning signs, its unaddressed presence unsettles us still, for what we see coming threatens to unravel not only our security but also our self-concepts, our ways of being and moving and describing our lives in this world. But what use is avoidance, when that world is passing away beneath our feet, and a new world is coming for us, urging us to pay attention? What then, when our attention is compromised by the last gasps of an old world, shiny but fragile, a fabrication whose repeated shocks signal a risky investment, built on sinking sand surrounded by rising waters? We can only shore up our defences for so long.

In a time of deep uncertainty, it is tempting to skip ahead to the ending. Some pray for the eschaton, ushering in a narrow salvation, damning the earth, along with all its varied life forms and topographies, to a fiery death prophesied incompletely from a holy land far away that few of us really know. Others acquiesce to a violent ending just the same, nihilistically naming inevitability and resigning themselves to absurdism: the theory that we live in a chaotic universe without meaning. Even the dreaded tragic ending can make us feel secure in the face of mystery. Those raised to play the prophet conjure this future as a kind of piety, as if forewarning others of the coming end would make more bearable – if certain – a still-incomprehensible loss of everything we have known and more we have not. But what if the grand, violent ending is not the certainty we imagine, unless we decide it will be?

Too many of us resist facing climate change by averting our gaze in the present or investing in various versions of a salvation narrative to run from a future we fear. The first is a salvation of humans from the earth (whether in heaven or on Mars). The second, a salvation of the earth *from* humans, nihilistically foretells our extinction with disquieting ecofascist admissions: 'humans are the virus' and 'the earth will be better off without us'. It is hard for many to imagine a future that does not ultimately divorce our fate from that of the earth. Both versions of the story take colonialism's exterminating excesses as given and capitalism's continuation as fact, while denying the possibility of the change that is needed in order for human life and planetary flourishing to coexist. They identify so completely with the very recent history of extractive capitalism, they cannot imagine human survival beyond it.

The manifold, far-reaching, yet imminent and intimate effects of this changing climate ask everything of us – ask us to suture ourselves to this shifting sand and move with it to ocean's depths. Though these times are charged with religious significance, it is not *belief* in the science that is at issue, as if merely repeating the warnings of experts would save us.[1] Will our descendants care that we *believed* the science, asks Jonathan Safran Foer, if our lives did not prove otherwise?[2] Far more than belief is required, and yet what is required is not simple. These last gasps of an old world are our invitation to pay attention, resist the temptation to look away or put false hope in a fabricated future, and heed the future being fabricated, now.

Whiteness, too, is bad faith. White supremacy and anthropogenic climate change are bedfellows, repopulating dangerous ideologies in persistent colonial habit. There is no unitary *anthropos* effecting this so-called Anthropocene; yet those of us who have traded culture for whiteness[3] as the privilege to consume the earth justify the ravaging by calling it natural, universal, 'sinful nature'. Though not its primary victims *by design*, some more than others are cogs in this Plantationocene, Capitalocene (and 'cene scene').[4] Whiteness is no privilege, but creates the conditions for sickness, illness and dis-*ease*, driving wedges between bodies and the soil from which they come.[5]

Though individual acts of racist violence do pervade and maintain this country's history, resurfacing now through the soil from which we cannot distance ourselves (the soil we need), white supremacy is a geography more than a problem with individuals, though it locates itself there, too. The kind of sin that pervades and maintains this architecture of oppression works at the level of the landscape. It is less a compounding of racist offences, more an indiscernible obedience to a mode of relation that goes on, through us, structuring our relations.

Bad faith is a lie to oneself,[6] used to avoid the implications of our actions. Yet, we know the consequences of decades of deception are coming. Indeed, they are already underway in deep ocean currents, where the embodied energy of denial cycles back to touch us, coming closer, creeping inside us and the comfort of our homes. Bad faith is precarious: our minds oscillate between consciousness and ignorance of the lies that sustain us. Everyday movements, as automatic as turning a key or flipping a switch, trigger violent combustions on unthinkable scales, as our actions are not merely our own but shared among many others, with unevenly distributed power unevenly distributing harm. It is these actions, mindless and mundane, that now tear at the fabric of our shared existence. Aggregated, they level ancient mountains and fell old-growth forests, obliterating respiring, resurrecting ecologies.

Humans in the carbon cycle

Carbon is everywhere, the building block of life. Carbon cycles recycle matter and transform energy, connecting us with all those who share our soil-borne life across our planetary history and into our planetary future.

When forcibly transformed and transported from earth to sky, carbon becomes animated with a life and deadly power of its own.[7] Mining Mesozoic graveyards, the dead we release from their dark underworlds haunt us in this world above. As we consume the bodies of those who came before to power and accelerate our own, we are living on borrowed time – time bought with the bodies of the dead whose solar time is distilled underground, and time stolen from the unborn.

Carbon has become a dirty word, an invisible villain. In our war against climate change, our task is to decarbonize as quickly as possible – to reduce, offset and sequester the atmospheric carbon responsible for all this cascading imbalance. We aim to shrink our carbon footprints, cut food miles as we localize food supply, and slash those travel miles most responsible for such irresponsible consumption. And yet carbon dioxide haunts us, stalking our every move.

The extent to which conscious consumers have internalized the concept of the carbon footprint is a victory for the fossil fuel industry. Calculate your carbon footprint, and be prepared for an immobilizing dose of despair, guilt and shame. This is the carbon footprint's sinister intention: to deflect blame for an unjust and fossil fuel-addicted world from the architects who profit from its maintenance, causing those who have no choice but to derive their sustenance from it to identify with it so completely they will not criticize it. Accusations of complicity silence those of us still motivated by the same shame and guilt we inherited from a version of Christianity where salvation is conceived as an individual achievement of purity in a fallen world.

It is impossible to be virtuous in the face of climate breakdown, but virtue is not the point. This predicament reveals the real problem. In America, even those without claim to a home, a car or a bank account have carbon footprints more than twice the size of the global average, not by direct consumption, but merely by existing within the world's hungriest economy.[8] Try as hard as some of us do to escape culpability, we live inside a deadly infrastructure.

For this reason, escaping culpability cannot be the goal.[9] If the problems are structural, the solutions must also be. Asking 'what can *I* do' is a good place to begin, but it leaves intact the too-common assumption that the problems with which we are faced collectively are commensurate with the scale of individual action. In truth, these scales are miscalibrated. While there is still so much we *can* do, seeing our lives and their impact at an individual scale obscures the power of the collectives of which we are part.

A farm is a living system, one that cycles carbon between the living and the dead. As a system, its constituent parts consume and transform resources to make resources available to others. The products of a farm include not only food but also soil and the carbon stored therein, recyclable and non-recyclable waste, as well as the material and economic impacts the farm exerts on surrounding communities and habitats. A farm can be judged according to its inputs and outputs, their ratios, relationship and the way these change over time. A sustainable farm does not consume more material or financial inputs than it produces over a similar timeframe. A regenerative farm builds, restores and sustains that farm's capacity to create what it relies upon as an ecosystem, slowing down and reversing extraction and depletion. These farms not only conserve but create fertile, living soil and clean water, decreasing their reliance on external inputs by designing spaces that produce what is needed in place.

Though a self-sustaining, regenerative agriculture is our goal, in many places it takes time and work to get there. A fellow farmer asks me about my reliance on plastic and how I imagine moving beyond the ubiquity of this toxic, polluting but extremely useful tool in organic farming. The need for plastic in organic agriculture reflects the compromised environment to which we belong: an environment in which oil is for now an abundant and subsidized resource, an environment in which improving water-use efficiency essentially requires the oil industry's polymer byproducts. We need drip tape and occultation tarps because water is scarce and invasive weed species are prevalent in the soils that agriculture has disturbed. We need landscape fabric because the economics of a small farm can't support the higher labour costs to hand weed, when plasticulture on so many other organic farms puts downward pressure on the price of produce that looks identical to shoppers in a store or at a stall. The problem of plastic in agriculture far exceeds the boundaries of the individual farm in which the said plastic is employed.

At the same time, plastic embodies a temporality, and is a trade-off in terms we can scarcely comprehend. Its short-term benefits can hardly justify its little-known, long-term consequences, if for no other reason than that we cannot think far enough into the future to which our use of plastic commits us. For how thoughtlessly and routinely we use plastics, we have an extremely limited ability to truthfully anticipate their effects, as they exist on timescales that are orders of magnitude larger and longer than we. While plastic makes our work possible in the short term, it will almost surely make other lives impossible in the long term.

Forever chemicals similarly trouble the historicities and timescales to which we are accustomed. Our minds, knowing constant change and short days, struggle to comprehend eternity, and yet our actions commit us to an eternal life of our own making, though one that is more of a haunting than a celestial paradise. PFAS, forever chemicals designed to make our lives just a little smoother, now travel not only through rivers and sea foam the world over, but in the bodies of all freshwater fish, and persist in the soils that feed our food. The soil that is life's resurrecting force can neither decompose nor resurrect these undying compounds. Our human bodies cannot digest what we manufacture but nor can we any longer escape.

It is no wonder that hopelessness abounds when the problems that today's students work to address become more intractable each day. There is little hope that their future will look anything like the present, and certainly unlike the past they study. They already disbelieve the rules of the game.

In compromised and compromising environments, as humans beings in this new carbon cycle, purity is a losing battle. We can filter water, filter air and eat clean, but our porous bodies are always communing with the toxins that constitute our world. Does this mean, then, that we ought to give up and give in to a world that ceaselessly reproduces all this injustice, and concern ourselves with enjoying the creature comforts that our toxic actions afford us so long as the earth can sustain them? What consequences await us in these decisions?

Climate hedonism

Each day, the land we hope to love slips away, becoming unrecognizable and contracting as sea levels rise. Development goes on sealing land, stopping its living decomposition and embalming its body, while encroaching dead zones overflow with toxins. Anxiously, we act in ways that further accelerate the contraction we fear, bringing closer the future from which we run. We rush, frenetically, to consume the world we hope to remember at the moment we fear it is passing away. We evade our own mortality, acting defiantly as if we have nothing but time. Rather than contract with an earth asking us to use its energy and our own more wisely, we hurry to maximize all we can extract for a little while longer, running out the clock ever faster as we spend down the time embodied in our energy sources and speed towards our own end.

The hedonic impulse seeks as its meaning in life the enjoyment of life, evading responsibility when that pleasure rests on the exploitation of others. More than heedlessly consuming what will not last, it is accelerating our consumption because we know it *cannot* last – not only outpacing earth's regenerative systems but taking actions that *compromise* those regenerative systems all the more. More than failing to respect limits, it reproduces narratives of endless growth to summon the false comfort of familiarity. The more we invest in a story that is coming to an end, the faster that end will come.

As grasping at the divine deadens the ineffable, grasping the earth turns living soil, a product inseparable from place, into fill dirt, mined and excavated, and idolized as property. We create the change we bemoan and yield power to what we fight. As places become scarce products in the minds of their consumers, those with purchasing power seeking elusive authenticity transform the living world they desire into commodity, like Midas's deadly touch. Small acts still stretch the limits within which we have always lived, accelerating unthinkably global feedback loops and haunting us with the signal breaks in normality they doubtless cause.

Even if we believe capitalism is passing away, so many of us invest in its continuation. We work jobs and seek paychecks, shunning long-term survival for short-term gains. We enjoy what we can, while we can, knowing change is coming, and speeding towards it. Climate hedonism is a fatalism that ushers in the ending it wishes to avoid.[10]

Structural violence, collective sin

Across the West in the Rocky Mountains, abandoned mines dot the hills we pass on the highway to the high country. Prospectors and profiteers are long gone and bankrupt, but their legacy remains for taxpayers today, who fund millions in cleanup to address acid mine drainage and widespread soil and water contamination each year. The modern state of Colorado was made by gold rushes, boring into living mountains to extract minerals whose traces remain in the soil: lead, arsenic, cadmium and zinc. Nowadays, these mines are relics and tourist destinations, as we recall the gritty horrors of those days. We do not hold those responsible accountable; we admire them to the extent we identify with them.

Historic and everyday violence works now without a primary perpetrator. Before being personalized and demonized, *ha-satan* was known as the adversary living in a realm, not of spiritual warfare, but within and through the human one. The violence at issue is not merely the discrete harm inflicted, as if the harm could be stopped if only it were identified. The harms that berate us and all our living neighbours are not so easy to see nor to *cease* because they are the manifold and multiplying products of grinding gears that so many of us spend our waking hours lubricating. Euphemisms distract us from the violence of today's extractive economies: the problem is 'emissions', not asthma rates in fence-line communities.[11] This kind of harm distributes moral agency across corporations and consumers – the violence of a slaughterhouse concentrates sites of harm all consumption hinges upon, but keeps it out of view.[12] The strict bifurcation between the clean and dirty, purity and compromise, at whose border the living becomes the product, implicates hundreds of individuals at work, though only a few witness the killing. But even among those who perpetrate violence, no individual is culpable. A slaughterhouse is a structural relation that accomplishes its goal while escaping moral implication. Each individual is a component belonging to a vast machinery and alienated from the act for which they are organized.

My grandfather's first job was in a horsekill factory. The

horses were made into dog food and glue, items found in any suburban home. The factory was a force pulling my grandfather out of poverty, away from the poor farm. The factory work helped him purchase a house, starting him on a long journey of upward mobility that would land him a comfortable life, eventually, far enough away from the stench of the kill floor of the factory and the dirt floor of his childhood home. Washing our hands, we are liable to forget, but olfactory memories trigger easily. The stench, he says, would linger on his clothing despite heavy laundering. He didn't pull the trigger, but the smell followed him home nonetheless.

Constructed worlds exert an undeniable pressure on us, delimiting and determining which actions we may take and which options we have. Built environments architect the possibilities of our lives, determining for us the impacts unleashed by our mere living. As individuals, our agency extends only so far. We can reduce our energy consumption or shower times, but it is much harder to change the source of energy delivered to us through the grid or determine how our water is treated or recycled.

Thinking with infrastructure is thinking at a scale proportional to that of the problems with which we are faced. Thinking at scale means thinking about ethics and morality beyond the scale of the individual. It requires differentiating between culpability and responsibility: taking responsibility even for that for which we are not culpable.

We are an infrastructure species, surviving within a world from which we are inseparable.[13] To *be perfect*[14] within a geography that causes us to sin against an earth we love and hope to preserve is a losing battle, when our environmental cues cause us repeatedly to *do not what we want*.[15] As an infrastructure species, our choices are not free. Moral action takes place within compromised and compromising environments, where the right course of action may not be entirely virtuous. While perfectionism occludes the powers that work against individual ambition and virtue, analysing the sources and limits of our shared and individual power enables us to navigate a complex moral landscape.

Urban planners know the power of spatial arrangements. Sitting in traffic, drivers wish for an obvious solution: build more lanes to speed up travel. But as lane expansion seeks to meet demand by increasing the supply of roadways, it also increases demand beyond what the increased supply can meet.[16] Put simply: we respond to the cues our environments give us. 'If you build it, they will come.' We are the traffic, after all.

Inside this infrastructure, individualistic fixations on purity and complicity no longer serve us. While the anxious shoulder responsibility for problems that far exceed them, the nostalgic shun responsibility by embracing guilt. Our actions and decisions can certainly curb the destruction we produce, but still so many of the decisions that make the environments we share are made not by us as individuals but by a world constructed by us and for us. The built environment is a limiting factor, the material with which we can work, but producing only a limited set of decisions available for us to make. Still, we do the best with what we've got. The carpenter works with a sloping floor or a room not-quite-square (as rooms in old houses tend to be), though the job would be easier were the circumstances otherwise. But to live without such constraints and such challenges is to live in a fictional world. Our work is to live well within a world whose movements we cannot determine or control.

Maintaining a farm is good practice in this regard. A farmer designs landscapes to accommodate needs of production, patterns of movement, and existing environmental limitations or legacies with efficiency in mind, making the wise use of resources more natural than laborious. Skilled farmers improve the function of natural systems so they can build soil and clean water. Rather than shrinking the impacts of individual action within an unjust and degrading environment, we meddle with our environments to set cooperative relations for mutual flourishing in motion.

If anything, sin is a geography we are locked inside more than a list of prohibited actions. It is not our choices but the highways we did not build dictating how we must safely get to work. It is the gas stations lining the highways with which we must fuel our lives. It is the electrical grid to which most of us must tie our homes. We belong to this geography – our identities are constructed within it – our homes, our neighbourhoods, the things, the food and the people we love. At our behest, but involuntarily, new highways, paved with our personal information, are being constructed all the time: our clicks logged in servers hoarding water somewhere, helping predictive tools make further predictions about our buying behaviour. Ultimately, it is these predictions that produce these behaviours, selling us what they convince us we want.

What we *do* matters, always reshaping and rearranging matter. Sin, seen structurally, affirms our status as social creatures. This complicates holiness projects, but may be more potent to transform living conditions on earth in ways that can save not only souls but species, not only humans but humus, not only Adam but *adamah*. Seeing sin as a built environment – not a condition of guilt from which we can be free in a word of absolution or denial, but a place we are called to transform – does not absolve humans of responsibility for it, but heightens our response-ability within it. It shifts the field of action, and our sense of agency, from carbon footprints and their tired individualism towards collective action. We must transform the places we live if we are to transform ourselves. We must rewild the places we live if we are to rewild ourselves. We must heal the places we live if we are to heal ourselves.

Our becoming is reciprocal: we are constantly being shaped by our environments, even as our living within those environments changes them. Even in degraded and exploited environments, can we find and cultivate life to make way for the living? Or will we assent to resentment, the paralysis of *ennui*, in an environment we see already as dead and doomed, thereby making it so?

The fire, inferno

30 December 2021

There are too many emergencies to bear. They eclipse and compound one another. I flew home from my home place last night. The winds were so heavy they knocked the plane off its course for a moment. I looked at Orion as I looked at the land, saying goodbye. *Orion.* The hunter. Everywhere and even before written record, the ancient ruler of the night sky, though this Orion does not exist except in the minds and storylines of those who perceive it from this earth we share (those stars, together, would take shape differently viewed from a different planet).[17] I thought about the lights below me, dotting the landscape with ceaseless development, how they shone brighter, almost, than the stars the plane flew nearer to, the air thick with light pollution from below. Yesterday, I was looking at dry land, wondering if it would be possible to farm and survive in this place I still so deeply love. Yesterday, I was optimistic. Today, I am not.

The same wind that kicked up the left wing of the plane, the same wind that I used to dance to inside as a child on that dry grass land, today blew 115 miles per hour, knocking over semi-trucks and power lines carrying coal-fired electricity, igniting grass and engulfing the homes of those we love. Engulfing *places* we love, the places that formed us. For years, we've bemoaned the endless sea of suburbs. Today, that sea is on fire.

The strip malls are on fire, too. Target and Costco, Tesla and Chuck E. Cheese shrouded in smoke while children, masked and sick, flee the illusory comforts those corporations sold. Here, at odds with the way of the land. The land that should be covered in a blanket of snow this time of year, and indeed awaits one within 24 hours, so says the optimistic forecast. But not here yet. Now, a dangerous drought persists, and the grass is still brown.

Will we rebuild this place the same way? Who will do the building? Already overburdened and with the supply chain strained, more houses feed the stress that caused this crisis in the first place. The stress of water scarcity is not going away.

Most of us don't see things this way, thinking the land's beauty is enough. Surely it is, but not for strip malls.

The emergency lines are choked with people offering donations, this last day of the tax year. They are asking people to stop. There is too much money here, too many people wanting too quickly to help to rebuild. But money can't put the fire out. I am told to pray for friends and family, to pray that the winds will stop. All those we love have left that place now. We wait to see what remains.

Compounding crises, confounding comprehension. Tens of thousands of neighbours evacuated to centres where the virus will spread. One church welcomes the Covid-positive and recovering. This is all too much for the nervous system already hypervigilant. This is why we numb.

Is God on our side (and whose side is that)? Is God in the fire, too?

What happens when you are already under a state of emergency, and another state of emergency is declared? Where – does – it – end?

Fire and flood. Biblical proportions. In these backyards of ours.

What's in this smoke, I wonder, burnt offering, but toxic? What does it smell like? Melting plastic entering soils where it will stay. Another scale of comprehension eclipses my small, daily demons.

The white world is ending, becoming too deadly. Time to get to work to make another world.

A week ago today – was it a premonition, a nudge? – ascending Sanitas, we saw smoke on the range. 'A grass fire,' a new acquaintance informed us.

Now, explosions of burning tyres. Christmas lights shattering. Christmas trees up in flames.

'The most destructive fire in state history.'

'What can I do?'

When we rebuild, will we rebuild with toxic chemicals, mined forests again? When will we learn?

No one knows how to see this land differently. No one sees another way.

After the fire

Years later, we replay the day's events. A permitted burn lost control on whipping winds. Downed power lines ignited dry, open acreage. Engulfing grasslands and creeping into denser cul-de-sacs (designed for privacy and not evacuation), the fire travelled along fence lines, torching the ember-touched homes they meant to separate in sequence. The grass caught the wind, caught the fence, caught the roofs. Homes spared held memory of thick black smoke requiring remediation, like the soils contaminated with all manner of plastics holding homes and lives together. After the fire, this land is more valuable – maybe only valuable – as lots than as soil so toxic. Now, again, it is only logical to rebuild. Lots sell for more and more to those eager to forget that the land must burn again. Insurance checks in the hands of those traumatized and haunted by flames replaying on eyelids – the triumphalism of taming again this nature by imposing upon it more, bigger, more climate-proof and protected real estate – are false assurances promising the security so desperately sought in a shifting and shaking and burning world.

Years later, we forget that these same ingredients that coalesced to produce this tragedy are still here, waiting for the conditions ripe for recombination. Perverse incentives fabricated by a capitalist economy silence this ground into submission once again. The risk we rightly fear has not gone away just because we've been through disaster once, but is redistributed through imperceptible rate hikes in insurance premiums. A low thrum of anxiety persists despite efforts to silence it, pervading the atmosphere of paradisal green. Wet springs and wet winters provide relief, lure us into thinking there is no problem to be solved. But green grass, when dried, becomes kindling, and we know the heat will melt snowpack and alter monsoons – that wind will whip through this grassland again as winter gets warmer still.

Climate apocalypse in the built environment

After disaster, recovery hopes for what is lost. Insurance markets cause people to rebuild in the same wild land–urban interface, despite the trauma and increased awareness of its risk. Financial incentives and mortgage debt cause victims to double down on bad investments, rebuilding the home that conferred prosperity on some to maintain and exacerbate this disparity of wealth we thought for a moment would be levelled with the homes.

Disaster capitalism seeks profit in times of loss, exploiting the chaos that comes when extreme weather strips places of their rules and governing structures, when whole worlds come undone.[18] In the chaos and grief, those who have lost everything question everything; those without stakes double down on the exploitative logic so responsible for so many disasters in the first place. After the fire, speculators offered victims cash for charred lots. These lots, empty parcels, still lifetimes of investment in real estate, must retain their market value despite the blatant and unchanged facts of ongoing risks. If not, the whole system collapses.

Up the hill where the water for these houses comes from, dry places with disappearing water become speculative investments. The 'law of the river' drives values up in an era of scarcity, when water is conceived not in terms of watersheds, but in terms of property. In the West, water is property, governed less as a shared resource than by the laws of competition: *first in time, first in right*, with only the time and rights of settlers validated. In the West, water is legally and physically separated from land, moved so far and between basins that groundwater cannot be recharged. In the West, water is wealth if you have it, and only affordable to the already-wealthy, who know too well that water is life. Those who have commodified this water use it to keep it their property, lest the water remain in the stream for the fish and be deemed 'abandoned'. The way water is used in the West to make our environments, electricity, alfalfa and lawns is a godlike creation whose stability is threatened.[19]

Apocalypse: unveiling. A word denoting not senseless death necessarily but, more fundamentally, a transformation in the way we see. The apocalypse we see as a threat is already here, though we run from it still. Maybe we will soon be redirected by changing currents, preserved for just a little while longer from the belly of the world slowly digesting us, until coughed up on the shores of our grief.

Post-apocalyptic visions of climate catastrophe surround us. Perhaps in this post-apocalypse we will become clear-eyed, able to face what stands before us already, but which so many of us are afraid to see: that our salvation is not *from* the land, but *to* and *for* it. There are no safe pastures in a contracting world. Threats to societies look different the world over, but they are pervasive, ever-present and only growing now. When our places are threatened by climate disasters, it causes us to want to stay, to love the land more in recognizing its aliveness. More because we hope to make it so. Climate disasters make us keenly aware of our inescapable interconnection to the places we are, reflecting back to us the disintegration we assume, enforce, enact. Stories and events once consigned to the realm of myth, tragedies of biblical proportions, are now increasingly commonplace, predicted by our best scientific models. Climate disasters reveal the spatial injustice of our built environments,[20] where neighbourhoods built in floodplains are hit hardest and worst. Climate shocks crack open and destabilize our built environments at the same time as they lay bare their rules.

Ongoing: a prayer

I have denied my own culpability, pursuing an impossible purity, but there is no purity to be found inside a compromised geography. There is no salvation from the place we find ourselves; our task is to make it different. We are co-creators, and our actions create the new world whether we see how or choose not to.

Give us eyes to see what we are doing, and capacities and vision to do what we must. Let us work not for our own salvation from a world that is passing away, but for those who will inhabit and make the world we are making today. Help us to see and know that the earth is alive, to honour and preserve its life in the ways we make ours. In and through our participation in life, may we make life go on.

Notes

1 Increasingly, the impacts of climate change stoke nationalistic fear, protectionism, isolationism, anti-immigrant sentiment and xenophobia. See Mike Hulme, 2009, *Why We Disagree about Climate Change: Understanding Controversy, Inaction and Opportunity*, Cambridge University Press.

2 Jonathan Safran Foer, 2019, *We Are the Weather: Saving the Planet Begins at Breakfast*, Penguin Canada.

3 See Resmaa Menakem, 2017, *My Grandmother's Hands: Racialized Trauma and the Pathway to Mending Our Hearts and Bodies*, Central Recovery Press, on 'bodies of culture'. Also James Baldwin on becoming white, or believing oneself to be white, quoted in Eddie S. Glaude Jr, 2020, *Begin Again: James Baldwin's America and Its Urgent Lessons for Our Own*, Crown, 2020.

4 Donna Haraway, 'Anthropocene, Capitalocene, Plantationocene, Chthulucene: Making Kin', *Environmental Humanities*, 6(1) (2015), pp. 159–65, https://doi.org/10.1215/22011919-3615934; Jason Moore (ed.), 2016, *Anthropocene or Capitalocene? Nature, History, and the Crisis of Capitalism*, PM Press. Andrew Curley and Sara Smith, 'The Cene Scene: Who Gets to Theorize Global Time and How Do We Center Indigenous and Black Futurities?', *Environment and Planning E: Nature and Space*, 7(1) (2023), pp. 166–88, https://doi.org/10.1177/25148486231173865.

5 'No threat has been more deadly and persistent for black and Indigenous peoples than the rule of white supremacy in the modern world. For over five hundred years, through the wedding of science and technology, white people have been exploiting nature and killing people of colour in every nook and cranny of the planet in the name of God and democracy.' James H. Cone, 'Whose Earth Is It, Anyway?' in *CrossCurrents*, 50 (1/2) (2000), pp. 36–46, p. 37.

6 Jean-Paul Sartre, 2018, *Being and Nothingness: An Essay in Phenomenological Ontology*, Routledge.

7 Timothy Mitchell, 2013, *Carbon Democracy: Political Power in the Age of Oil*, Verso Books.

8 Timothy Gutowski et al., 2008, 'Environmental Life Style Analysis (ELSA)', in *2008 IEEE International Symposium on Electronics and the Environment*, San Francisco, pp. 1–5.

9 Alexis Shotwell, 2016, *Against Purity: Living Ethically in Compromised Times*, University of Minnesota Press.

10 See Jenny Odell on declinism, 'the belief that a once-stable society

is headed for an inevitable and irreversible doom'. Jenny Odell, 2023, *Saving Time: Discovering a Life beyond Productivity Culture*, Random House Publishing Group, p. 157.

11 Rob Nixon, 2011, *Slow Violence and the Environmentalism of the Poor*, Harvard University Press.

12 Timothy Pachirat, 2011, *Every Twelve Seconds: Industrialized Slaughter and the Politics of Sight*, Yale University Press.

13 Jedediah Purdy, 2021, *This Land Is Our Land: The Struggle for a New Commonwealth*, Princeton University Press, p. 88.

14 Matthew 5.48.

15 Romans 7.15–20.

16 Jeff Speck, 2013, *Walkable City: How Downtown Can Save America, One Step at a Time*, Macmillan.

17 Tyson Yunkaporta, 2020, *Sand Talk: How Indigenous Thinking Can Save the World*, HarperCollins.

18 Naomi Klein, 2010, *The Shock Doctrine: The Rise of Disaster Capitalism*, Henry Holt and Company.

19 Dorothee Soelle reminds us that we are the way God works in the world. Dorothee Soelle, 2006, *Dorothee Soelle: Essential Writings*, Orbis Books, p. 78. 'In reality everything relating to the preservation of this earth depends on the lives and behaviour of people in the rich world. We are involved; we are responsible' (p. 77).

20 Edward W. Soja, 2010, *Seeking Spatial Justice*, University of Minnesota Press.

5

Becoming Place, Fermenting Culture

Fall equinox

Late summer is a long, golden hour. The peak of all the season's productivity foreshadows its loss as nights start to cool. Just at that moment summer's light peaks, already it begins its descent into darkness. Since this June, the nights have been growing, at first imperceptibly, then suddenly. Though we love the light, in overflowing times we are relieved that nothing lasts forever – not the long winter of waiting, nor summer's utter exhaustion. Pocked skin on these first cool nights of fall signal a world's ending – like peak oil, peak stuff signals a turn away from an intensity the earth will not forever bear. It is in these last gasps that our vision is split – looking back while looking ahead. At this juncture we perceive a shift that's been happening under our feet all along, from growth to decay. The smell of sweet rot from the first decomposing leaves tells us the end is coming. It would be foolish to turn the other way, against the seasons, planting when the sunlight is retreating. Seeds planted now will not grow large until spring anyway, if their plants survive the winter dormant, as fall days count less than summer's implied on a seed packet. We are invited now to the work that accompanies the season's end and its last harvests. We welcome the beginning this end foretells: we move not along an axis, but in a circle.

This time of year, as petrichor mixes with the slant light and the green, the photosynthetic, turns from plant-feeding tissue to tissue-feeding plant, the bounded individuality of the self-contained and recognizable fades into mere carbohydrate. The soil this decomposition feeds stores food ready for next year's plants, as we store the soil's food and wait for next year's tending.

Practice makes process

At certain latitudes, cultures coalesce around the tasks associated with surviving winter. The foods with which we mark seasonal shifts also ensure our preparedness for the cold and dark ahead. The celebration and maintenance of the season's abundance go hand in hand. Winter is a time for making and preserving cultures, too. We partner with unseen lives we rely on for the culturing, transforming food from fresh to cured. Even as our cultural and preservative actions extend the shelf life of plant lives stored in earthen and limestone cellars to keep us fed when the day's light wanes, these activities form the basis of the food cultures through which place comes to taste.

It is not the produce but the process that is the outcome of the labour that tends and sustains a living system. Practice makes not perfection but process. Because plant life is always on its way towards rot and cannot be stored except as it lives through the bodies of those it feeds, the produce that is the product of a growing season can never last. Though land's produce commodified and financialized may be hoarded, its value transfixed through innumerable transformations, the produce of the land is more valuable shared. A farmer's wealth turns to rot in short time,[1] as if by design in a world where all humans need daily bread and every human has a finite body to limit their consumption. Agricultural work is a kind of caretaking, reproductive labour never finished. What it makes goes away; its use is to maintain for a little while longer the life of the soil through the lives of those it feeds. When produce is transformed to money, the income a farm generates goes back into its operation to make more of the same: more life through life, in a circle.

The produce of our labour is not the sole outcome of farm work or food production. These are valuable for only the brief moment of their enjoyment. Embodying the process is its own outcome, teaching lessons that make possible the continuation of processes refined by practice. When we work with our hands, we make modifications to make processes smoother and more pleasant. We learn to keep close the tools we use repeatedly, and we anticipate which ones we'll need ahead of time. We remember recipes and move through them more quickly with repetition. We make jigs and storyboards so our rows are uniform. We find easier ways to complete repetitive tasks – bunching onions or carrots – and learn shortcuts so we can do more with less. Season after season, we adopt new lessons in a process that makes the system keep working to keep feeding. The work is never 'done' as we might like to imagine, but is its own end. Whatever progress we achieve in a season, we start back at the beginning next time, bringing with us only the lessons and the strategies we've learned. *Practice makes process*: the work that is needed to live is continuous so long as we are living.

Growing food allows us to apprehend the true costs of our lives, whether those costs are ours to bear or those we externalize to others. It is humbling to know what a salad costs; the difficulty of its production will make you feel small, especially in a world where cheap food born of cheapened labour is abundant. Grown alone, a salad takes days of soil preparation, tillage, soil testing and amendment, months of planning to get the timing right, and weeks of cultivation by hand so that tender leaves can grow larger than weeds. Hours of harvesting, washing and packing, all for a handful of calories and a product whose best hope is to be enjoyed very briefly, but is often forgotten and left to rot, and in either case is mostly taken for granted. A farmer knows – their body remembers – the true costs of eating, whether the cost is one's own time and energy converted from the last meal grown by someone else's hands, or the same quantity of energy derived from fossil fuels made of meals of ancient animals millennia ago, fuelling engines whose embodied energy accelerates time in more ways than one.

Farming helps me come to terms with the fact of life's impermanence, which might seem nihilistic in a culture that prizes stability and control. The fact that nothing lasts forever can cause discomfort, since this implies our mortality, too. While the religious imagery of the Eucharist evokes a divine and unchanging eternity, the elements of that meal show us an eternal life we know already: not fixed or stable but shared between many. Maybe the lesson of that meal is not so different from the lessons of the meals we eat daily. Maybe the sacrifice that allows us to live is less of a cosmic barter between sinful humans and an angry god, and more like every other holy meal. Maybe every sacrifice – of plant, of animal, of neighbour – is what already sustains our eternal life collectively as a continuous communion.

As a continuously modified living system, the farm in many ways takes care of itself. Though I like to imagine that the farm requires my constant attention and care in order to justify the attention and care I religiously devote to it, my agency is only one factor at play. A farmer's role is not to control the way that life unfolds, but to design environments and feedback loops that foster vitality and cooperation between many more living entities. Though my mind imposes a mechanistic view, the processes unfolding are never entirely predictable. And yet, observation provides the data I need to adjust the inputs, arrangements and timing I try next.

Preserving culture

Like the hands of the farmer, the hand of the fermenter begins a process that unfolds on its own. We select the ingredients, set up a process inside a container and impart to this environment the bacteria living on our skin. While salt inhibits the growth of certain bacteria, lactobacilli living on the skin of fruits, vegetables and humans multiply. Temperature determines which microbes thrive and how quickly they multiply, and wild yeasts collected from thin air add depth of flavour. The fermenter sets the process in motion – combining the ingredients in a vessel and a place – but the living system of which the fermenter is merely a part has a life of its own, created by the interactions between the lives of many. Once set in motion, the process of this eating, feeding and communing sustains itself.

At this point in the season, my work shifts from the process of production that is facilitated cooperation between soil microbes, water and sunlight and moves indoors, to a production process that is a different kind of facilitation: between microbes, yeasts and the sugars and carbohydrates that now embody the summer's waning sunshine energy. These activities mirror one another: while the fresh produce of my labour feeds my human neighbours throughout the season, in fermentation I feed the land's produce to still more others, though these neighbours are unseen. As days get shorter, my attention turns to feeding and nurturing the microscopic, symbiotic bacteria and yeast, who in consuming my sugary offerings exude enzymes that return the favour: lending me the microflora with whom I share gut space that aid my digestion and unlock nutrients, as well as preserving the food I've grown by further transforming it, preserving it from the rot wrought by decomposing bacteria by encouraging preservative bacteria to make a home there instead. Eating is constant – what is not consumed by humans is still inevitably consumed, by animals or by microorganisms which break down food to soil or keep food from soil for a little longer and for me.

Saint Basil instructs us that the bread we hold always belongs to the hungry; that which moulds and rots belongs to those who have need. Our decomposing conspirators remind us that the land's produce is not to be hoarded. All of us – plant, animal, bacteria – are only here momentarily, and only sustained through the time we are given, through the food that is itself a distillation of the time sunshine offers. Hoarding takes living land sustaining living out of time. What is not offered as food for others denies that life to others, hoarding time that is ours to share but not ours to keep.[2]

Fermentation preserves what land gives on the shelf by feeding microscopic collaborators, making food not less but more alive. And it is this living food that makes our lives go on. Life here is not a zero-sum game: one life won by another lost, or one fed by another dead. It is *life* than makes life go on. Life as labour, life as love, life as the time one gives, life as the time we share.

Arts of fermentation are ubiquitous, guiding processes of decay away from sickening rot towards novel tastes the world over. Not only do these tastes serve our survival and enjoyment, they make culture, memory and the internal worlds that shape immune function and cognition. Fermentation is an ancient practice, but it survives only as a living one, and its permutations are therefore endless. Every ferment comes from somewhere, but every ferment only survives as it travels.[3] As it covers ground, it transforms in relation to new ground it finds.

Fermentation is equally science and art. On many levels, it is complex and mysterious, and yet it is also the most basic and ubiquitous technology for preserving human communities through winter while transforming human cultures through food. Fermentation happens through processes both simple and complex passed down over time. Fermentation also happens on its own, inevitably, as fruit sugars turn to alcohol. Fermentation is the simplest way we humans make our foods more nutritious, more delicious and safer.[4] Fermentation unlocks nutrients, conveying enzymes and bacteria to help us digest food. Fermentation fundamentally changes the way food tastes, adding the depth of distinctive and irreplaceable umami. Fermentation is responsible for the survival of our food cultures, but also necessary for our own.

Fermentation is the magic of transformation, a collaborative, multispecies process of making environments to make life in ways that add up to mutual flourishing. The benefits of fermentation's mutualisms are not proprietary nor mutually exclusive, but additive: as microbes find new homes, humans find new tastes. All this because committed individuals, exercising their knowledge and care, pay attention to patterns of change enough to work with them. We watch for bubbly signs of life and continue to feed that life – jumping in, lending a hand, creating environments to make new worlds, new life, possible.

Like agriculture, fermentation is a cultural practice that is always changing us back. Speaking of soil work, María Puig de la Bellacasa writes of the haptic technologies involved. She implies that these processes are uniquely and mutually formative: 'We can see without being seen, but can we touch without being touched?'[5] As what we touch touches us back, the hands with which we touch are changed. The calluses my hands form in response to the work they perform make the work of tilling, tractoring, trellising all the easier. Hands rough to the touch carry the soil bacteria I am unable to rinse from beneath my fingernails first into the ferment, then into my belly, and my inner world communes with the outer world I tend through *son mat* ('hand taste').[6]

As the work of growing food transitions to the work of preserving food grown, it strikes me that both regenerative agriculture and wild fermentation rely heavily on microbial partnerships. This causes me to ask, what is the relationship between compost and fermentation? Both move me from a place of tired rigidity towards an open-ended future – one not defined by the doubts, fear and constraints in which my mind is so often enmired. What I learn, through practising both, is that both are processes of transition, transformation, by which we forge partnerships with small ones – microbes and fungi – who digest the dead – the world – in ways we cannot on our own, to feed and nurture the living. These small ones, the land's internal metabolism reconfiguring its biomass, digest the weight of a world that can feel heavy. In our kitchens and gardens, our work is both to break down and to build: breaking down what we cannot bear, building soil and flavour in its place.

Both compost and fermentation are ubiquitous. Both are a durable, refined and indispensable process of microbial collaboration with which we are co-evolved. Both indelibly shape our cultures and our places, yielding terroir. These actions simultaneously build soil and culture, which come to taste in place. Though different processes with distinct ends, compost and fermentation both harness the power of microbial life to transform individual plant and animal lives into near unrecognizability. Just as the product of composting's end bears no resemblance to its constitutive parts, in fermentative processes, foods are entirely remade, producing novel tastes distinct from their initial ingredients. In fermentation, microbe, yeast, time and temperature are crucial ingredients, too, in relationship yielding flavour not possible in isolation and extending the end date of food that would otherwise return more quickly to rot. While fermentation curbs the growth of decomposing bacteria by selectively breeding for preservative ones, both compost and fermentation transform soil-borne life in nutritious and delicious ways. While one's goal is degradation, the other's is preservation. Breakdown is managed to produce the products that make our lives go on, the soil and the culinary traditions they bear.

Both compost and fermentation are useful processes, both for conceiving the ways in which we are not merely individuals and for inviting us into practices that exemplify that reality. Both compost and fermentation show us that we are not forever self-contained, but interconnected with a living earth that has the power to save us *and* the power to undo us. Figuratively and literally, compost and fermentation break down the self-protective barriers upholding individualism with enzymes and fungi, bacteria and yeasts. While Pasteurian politics have conditioned us to accept as normal the antibacterial practices that erect a fictive barrier between the body and a too-lively world, we are better in and *as* communities than we are in isolation.[7]

Both compost and fermentation harness time and temperature as ingredients. The art and science of both are to adjust labour and material inputs to ever-shifting environmental realities. Bacteria respond to ambient temperatures: becoming activated, more numerous and hungrier in the brew vat. In the compost pile, temperature directs the ratios and composition of mesophilic and thermophilic bacteria, who take shifts throughout decomposition's oscillations.

These time-honoured processes are so deeply embedded in our culinary traditions that we no longer recognize them as such. A world without fermentation is a world without coffee, chocolate, bread and cheese, not to mention wine in its social *and* sacramental uses. Still, even avid consumers of fermented foods turn squeamish when considering their production in a modern world where food safety and sanitation are associated with the *anti*-microbial and health departments struggle to understand and regulate the uses of older food safety technologies.

A homework assignment encouraged students to investigate their family's inherited culinary traditions for evidence of microbial activity and bring to the farm a fermented food and its story to share with the class. Responses to this assignment varied: some were practised, some were sceptics and still others were amazed at the microbial agency hiding in plain sight. For many, the task reconnected them more intimately to the foods they loved – sweet breads and yogurt – for a fuller understanding of the processes involved. Some discovered fermentation at work in unsuspected places, recreating the tepache of street vendors in Mexico.[8] Others turned up their noses at the funkier versions of sauerkraut that made their way to the table in the barn that day.

Getting involved in fermentation reminds us that the world is fundamentally alive, that we are not the only agents or sentient beings forging creative collaborations in response to changing environmental conditions. On our own, we do not create life, but merely preserve, enhance and host it. The world inside our bodies is similarly raucous, and the microbiome fed by the probiotics produced from living food affects our brain chemistry, we now know. We are not the intelligent individuals we are without the microscopic worlds we carry and inhabit. We are not our own, but shaped by the microbes more numerous in us than our own cells.[9]

What we touch touches us back.[10] Our hands do not control, but arrange, impart and inoculate an already-living world with yet more life living on our skin, mixing with the lives carried on the skin of fruits. A sourdough culture gets a kick start from the skin of an unwashed grape. Skin is the soil of worlds at other scales, and our skin is likewise less a barrier than an interface. The microbiome of our bodies and the microbiome of the soil talk to each other. Both host the incomprehensible biodiversity and indispensable symbioses that are the foundation of our lives together.

Our culinary traditions impart to us the wisdom that preserving life requires not fighting against a living world to make it less alive, but cooperating with a living world to create the kinds of life for which we hope.[11]

Arts of fermentation do theological work, too: upending the human exceptionalism inherited from Christian beliefs that separate a saved human soul from an inferior and death-bound world. And yet the elements are there on the table: those who produce life-giving bread and wine through partnering with a very alive world see in the sacrament that eternal life is not merely a future state but also a present reality, inherited from the past. Eating and sharing the life of a living earth join our lives to this already-eternal.

Resurrection is an environmental reality, not possible in isolation. On earth as in heaven, we are resurrected, not as individual, self-contained bodies, but like this: in the brew vat, sugars from cane feed *lactobacillus acidophilus*, which produces lactic acid to feed *bifidobacterium bifidium*. This chain reaction embedded in heterolactic fermentation processes makes the food that feeds our gut microbiome and preserves harvests to sustain us through winter.

Space and time

With fermentation, time and temperature are themselves ingredients affecting the final product. Over time, sourness and acidity become more pronounced, but at different rates depending on the season. Sour pickles pickle faster in the summer, when they're fresh. Sourdough requires more patience in winter, when microbial activity slows in the soil and in the kitchen alike.

The relationship between time and temperature goes beyond the recipe, for fermentation is also a way of extending time, preserving summer's frenetic pace driven by abundant solar energy for the slower season ahead. Peak sunlight brings peak produce ripe for fermentation in midsummer to extend shelf life before temperatures wane. Slowly, we descend into the darkness of winter with the help of our preservative friends.

Time and temperature work in tandem, but they also change one another: the higher the temperature, the shorter the time.

Fermentation happens faster and more explosively when the weather is hot, mirroring our societal temperature in a warming climate. The word 'fermentation' comes from the Latin *fervere*: to boil. Early experimenters were mystified by the enigmatic force causing fruit juice to bubble without heat. Today, as oceans boil and permafrost thaws, we witness more and more mysterious forces awakened by this new environment with its new ambient temperatures, and more and more of us are waking up to a warming world. Ferment also suggests *foment*, implying and unleashing the unrest to which we are also awakening: the higher the global temperature, the shorter the time we have to work to avoid catastrophe.

A warming world breeds violence, and not only for human societies, when homicide rates increase alongside the discomfort, irritation and resource scarcity that rising temperatures bring.[12] A warming world is slow violence,[13] with growing threats of extinction for innumerable others, as life ways and flight ways[14] adapted to temperature norms are thrown out of whack by broken records year after year. If fermentation has been for humans a way to slow the time of decomposition each winter, fermentative processes now show time's acceleration in a world of rising temperatures, where the relationship between time and temperature continues to evolve. It is getting hotter. We are running out of time.

We won't be able to run from the new world being created. As fermentation shows us, we are inextricably part of this world and its processes. The foment in the ferment is growing fast. Soil waking to an earlier spring is a microbial response to a warmer world. Perhaps accelerationism is ours, as apocalyptic narratives are our way of storying and recalibrating to this weirding. We, too, are fermenting.

We are told continually that we are headed for the worst, that we must change to avoid catastrophe. And yet we are changing continuously. Even as things heat up to the point of discomfort and cause us to wish for the end of the world we imagine, could something good come out of this brew? Prepping our bunkers with dead foods preserved by industrial canning processes and ultra-high-temperature pasteurization is one way to preserve lives from foodborne illnesses. While I am no raw milk evangelist, it also strikes me that, in industrial systems, preservation involves making living foods dead: setting up antagonisms and maintaining divisions, even if we preserve our lives individually for a while.

As long as earth grows food-producing plants, human cultures are sustained. Dystopian visions predicting the survival of nuclear winter by extra-planetary colonization miss the opportunity here, now: to ferment in this time, together – to make something new as we feed one another.

The weight of the world

I am thinking very often of this heavy *technosphere*:[15] the weight of human *techne*, these systems of collective life support forged of concrete and steel. The technosphere is more than a 'footprint', and more like the path it walks: the grids and roads and mines and transformers, asphalt and guardrails and easements and jetways, scaffolding and freight trains and cargo ships anchoring us to a built environment whose referent and source is still and always the natural world. The weight of the human-modified artificial habitat that sustains human life today is an incomprehensible 30 trillion tons, meaning that, for each one of us there exists 4,000 tons of human-built life support.[16] The technosphere is agriculture, farms and livestock, roads, concrete buildings and Styrofoam – not only what we, individually, realize we use, but all that is used, erected and manufactured on our behalf. The technosphere dwarfs all talk of footprints. At this scale, we see we act upon the world together, and far more as collectives than as individuals.

Earth lives and breathes soil, air and water, like us. This civilization has become skilled at transforming soil-borne elements to environments that do not respirate or decompose. Concrete alchemized with steel reinforcements sources sand from river bottoms, where dredging alters ecologies doubly: in the rivers, where sand's removal robs the river of primary feeders; and above the soil, where transformed concrete fixes environments in time by removing them from space. Built environments seek stability, uniformity and ease: asphalt allows us to move fast over complications unthinking, erasing earthly implication to accommodate speed. An environment built from the pieces of environments elsewhere does not live – interrupt – the same.

Animal domestication has greatly altered ecologies. European settlers used agriculture to dispossess and build a nation, transforming the 'wasteland' they saw. In Iowa, scarcely 1 per cent of that state's landmass has been spared from settlers' monocultural transformations.[17] Grazing cattle were (and are) instruments of Western settlement, replacing bison whose wallows create pollinator habitat with their domesticated substitute, allowing homesteaders to carve out an agrarian living and associated land claims despite the aridity west of the hundredth meridian. Prairies, wetlands, savannas and forests are now endless fields of corn and soy for animal feed. The animal companions we feed are selected to suit our tastes,[18] and now comprise 60 per cent of all mammals by weight, leaving just 4 per cent non-human, non-domesticated and wild.

Compared to the biomass of terrestrial plants, fungi, and bacteria from the rhizosphere to the sea floor that weaves the land together, animals account for a small percentage of the total weight of the world, and yet our dominance among mammals like us is nonetheless unsettling. Unsettling, too, is the loss of biodiversity in dominant food systems – humans rely on just three of tens of thousands of edible crops – corn, wheat and rice – to meet roughly half of our caloric needs.[19] The world humans have built shrinks biodiversity in other kingdoms.[20]

The technosphere is heavy on the earth, erecting barriers between us and the soil created by our making and unmaking and interrupting decomposition. It sanitizes our microbiome by separating us from soil creatures with whom we've co-evolved. Separation from soil affects our immune function but also our perception of our place in the natural world and the sources of our lives.

Certain patterns of land use and settlement have diminished the biodiversity of land and foodways, but this hasn't always been the case.[21] While the forms that growing and eating take can compromise the biodiverse communities of living landscapes, how we eat can also grow, share and create biodiverse food webs, weaving connections across the artificial borders between humans and the rest of the living world sustaining our living.

In the soil, bacteria and fungi constitute a soil microbiome and make possible advanced forms of communication and resource-sharing among species. I am cultivating this microbiome with new practices and old principles, brewing tea to feed the underground, invisible world. I talk to farmers who place wooden boxes of white rice in the forest floor, waiting for fungal partners to weave their webs through the substrate, which is then removed and transformed into an amendment for an elsewhere field. What get called weeds offer back to the soil what the soil needs. Weeds are communicators and vectors, over time restoring soil.[22] Farmers are harvesting these weeds to create nutrient-rich extracts. The minerals these weeds take up are redistributed within the soil by design. My actions can accelerate this process, mimicking decades of nutrient cycling in a season's time. I make compost tea in my bubbler, feeding the microbes of vermicompost with humic acid and kelp to stimulate more microbial growth in the brew vat. I spray this tea on the leaves of plants to strengthen their immune systems. I am harnessing and stemming breakdown with the fermentative technologies I employ, in partnership with the microbes I cannot live without.

There are ways of living in a damaged world that cause further harm by further shrinking biodiversity. There are other ways of living in a damaged world that seek to reverse these trends by cultivating liveliness. With every action, we have a choice: whether to aid, assist, cultivate and remediate or to make this work harder for those who will come after us. Every action has an ecological impact: respirating, eating, decomposing. We can call this way of concrete and climate apocalypse inevitable, or we can practise surviving this moment in planetary history by cultivating partnerships with other species, as we have always done to survive.

To ferment is to multiply biodiversity. To ferment is also to practise surviving amid messiness and complication, recovering older technologies for preserving life.[23] To ferment is to digest individuality, which is good practice given where we are as a species. So much of the world of human making is designed to *not* be broken down.

To ferment is to feed the world – to feed a microscopic world I cannot see. It is an act of faith that a world beyond my experience exists, and in acting upon that faith I find evidence of things not seen, in sourdough rising and sauerkraut bubbling, respirating carbon dioxide. Fermentation is a practice that affirms for me the aliveness of the world and seeks to participate in and grow that aliveness to promote mutual flourishing. In so many ways, it is antithetical to the practices that see the world's aliveness, change and instability as a threat to neutralize through practices of enforced stability: food preservation, shoreline stabilization, sterilization. Ironically, these efforts to fight the living world by deadening it almost always backfire: creating pandemics and antibiotic resistance, accelerating the severity of natural disasters and making recovery from them more difficult, creating chemical dependencies for degraded and near-death soils that generate first eutrophication and then the dead zones where those chemical inputs travel and aggregate. Despite our best efforts to control the living world, the living world slips out of our control, to control, determine and delimit the possibilities of our present and future lives. Partnering with the living world is and always has been the best and only way to survive. The only security we have is in relationship.

Fermentation feeds the world by facilitating beneficial forms of breakdown, harnessing rather than sanitizing microbial life, feeding the metabolism by which earth is transformed to food and back again. Industrial culture starves the world by erecting barriers that interfere with land's metabolism – protecting the built environment from decay to preserve living land as stable property. Industrial culture functions under the assumption – and with the desire – that the earth be dead, that matter be inert, because it loves the money it derives from the living world more than life itself. It makes money out of death, money as a form of death.[24] It makes a concrete-heavy technosphere that will not easily be broken down and does not commune with microorganisms to decompose or preserve. And yet, inside these processes of commodification, the living world breaks through. Erosion and earthquake smooth down and break down technospheric impositions. As any builder knows, homes are built not of widgets but of living elements – trees continue to breathe, shrink, crack and weep sap even after being milled into framing members. Everything we hold becomes earth again.

If the technosphere is the weight of the world, rearranged in ways the world cannot as readily digest, can we rearrange the world's matter and its flows to recover the relationality that is its health? Can we do this without the patterned attempts to grasp, hold and derive profit from a living, regenerating earth as equity or property? Though we live in a context of constrained choices and freedom, in the wake of the metabolic rift[25] that decouples rural production from urban consumption in ways that proliferate landfills of fictive 'aways', perhaps we can still find and forge alternative systems that feed our economic excess to the small ones we've neglected, to digest this technosphere with the help of the nonhuman and microscopic. With fungi, mobilizing latent toxins but also remediating what we can't break down alone.[26] Our touch may contaminate – *con tangere* – but also make sites of fruitful and collaborative interaction. We are not in control, but conspirators.

Transformation: a prayer

Relinquishing the desire for control, I am coming to terms with a growing reality. Letting go of inherited entitlements to the comfort of consuming earth's resources, my work is to break down with the earth more than break the earth down to suit fantasies. These microbes make us human, more than our distance from them. We are not minds but bodies, and as bodies, not our own. We respond to the desires of many unseen. We are not gods, sovereign over reality, but God is with all of us, together, in our pattern of relation. When we 'go with our gut', we do not go alone.

What can we, together, no longer digest? What will we, together, need to break down? What will we, together, work to preserve, to carry us through this growing darkness ahead? Can we slow our march towards death as our ancestors did, resuscitating older practices for slowing down time?

To feed is to be fed, to be fed is to feed. Eating is not a transaction but a communion. When Christ dies Christ feeds others, but not as substitution. Life is continuance, not living and dying for or in spite of but living and dying through, exchanging matter and sharing space eternally. This is not a violent substitutionary atonement, in which a predatory or vindictive death is excused as a necessary part of life. Opting out of the zero-sum game, we are rescued from individuality instead. Is that not what this Christ taught us? We live by feeding others, even as we are fed by still others. We are the earth's metabolism. Our surrender is not defeat but acceptance that our life – its source, its consequences – is far more expansive than the bounds of our skin. Our skin does not contain self-stable, shelf-stable identities, but interfaces with a world teeming with life, and it is this that allows our lives to go on.

May we not impede this exchange, turning life into property, life into an impossible stability, life into death. Let our living and our dying feed a living world eternally instead.

Notes

1 James 5.2.

2 Thank you to my friend Teagan, who helped me see the ways that hoarding money is a way of hoarding another's labour-time.

3 Sandor Ellix Katz, 2020, *Fermentation as Metaphor*, Chelsea Green Publishing, p. 54.

4 Katz, *Fermentation as Metaphor*, p. 106.

5 María Puig de la Bellacasa, 2017, 'Touching Visions', in *Matters of Care: Speculative Ethics in More than Human Worlds*, 3rd edn, University of Minnesota Press, pp. 95–122, p. 97.

6 René Redzepi and David Zilber, 2018, *The Noma Guide to Fermentation: Including Koji, Kombuchas, Shoyus, Misos, Vinegars, Garums, Lacto-Ferments, and Black Fruits and Vegetables*, Artisan, 2018.

7 Aminah Al-Attas Bradford, 2021, 'Symbiotic Grace: Holobiont Theology in the Age of the Microbe', Doctor of Theology, Duke University, https://hdl.handle.net/10161/24460, accessed 09.06.2025.

8 César Ojeda-Linares et al., 'Traditional Fermented Beverages of Mexico: A Biocultural Unseen Foodscape', *Foods*, 10(10), 2390 (2021), https://doi.org/10.3390/foods10102390.

9 Ed Yong, 2016, *I Contain Multitudes: The Microbes Within Us and a Grander View of Life*, Ecco.

10 For a discussion of haptic technologies, see Puig de la Bellacasa, 'Touching Visions'.

11 See, for example, Samuel Ariyo Okaiyeto et al., 'Antibiotic Resistant Bacteria in Food Systems: Current Status, Resistance Mechanisms, and Mitigation Strategies', *Agriculture Communications*, 2(1), 100027 (2024), https://doi.org/10.1016/j.agrcom.2024.100027.

12 Christopher P. Barlett et al., 'Hot Temperatures and Even Hotter Tempers: Sociological Mediators in the Relationship between Global Climate Change and Homicide', *Psychology of Violence*, 10(1) (2020), pp. 1–7, https://doi.org/10.1037/vio0000235.

13 Rob Nixon, 2011, *Slow Violence and the Environmentalism of the Poor*, Harvard University Press.

14 Thom van Dooren, 2014, *Flight Ways: Life and Loss at the Edge of Extinction*, Columbia University Press.

15 Peter Haff, 'Humans and Technology in the Anthropocene: Six Rules', *The Anthropocene Review*, 1(2) (2014), pp. 126–36, https://doi.org/10.1177/2053019614530575.

16 Jedediah Purdy, 2021, *This Land Is Our Land: The Struggle for a New Commonwealth*, Princeton University Press, pp. 22, 78.

17 'Science from Iowa's Prairies', *Science Friday*, 3 May 2024, https://www.sciencefriday.com/segments/iowa-prairie-science/, accessed 09.06.2025.

18 Michael Pollan, 2003, *The Botany of Desire: A Plant's-Eye View of the World*, Bloomsbury.

19 Colin K. Khoury et al., 'Increasing Homogeneity in Global Food Supplies and the Implications for Food Security', *Proceedings of the National Academy of Sciences*, 111(11) (2014), pp. 4001–6, https://doi.org/10.1073/pnas.1313490111.

20 Martin J. Head et al., 2021, "The Great Acceleration Is Real and Provides a Quantitative Basis for the Proposed Anthropocene Series/Epoch," *Episodes Journal of International Geoscience*, 45(4), pp. 359–76, https://doi.org/10.18814/epiiugs/2021/021031.

21 Vandana Shiva, 1993, *Monocultures of the Mind: Perspectives on Biodiversity and Biotechnology*, Palgrave Macmillan.

22 Nicole Masters, 2019, *For the Love of Soil: Strategies to Regenerate Our Food Production Systems*, Integrity Soils Limited.

23 Nicola Twilley, 2024, *Frostbite: How Refrigeration Changed Our Food, Our Planet, and Ourselves*, Penguin.

24 Devin Singh, 2018, *Divine Currency: The Theological Power of Money in the West*, Stanford University Press.

25 John Bellamy Foster, 'Marx's Theory of Metabolic Rift: Classical Foundations for Environmental Sociology', *American Journal of Sociology*, 105(2) (1999), pp. 366–405, https://doi.org/10.1086/210315.

26 Harbhajan Singh, 2006, *Mycoremediation: Fungal Bioremediation*, John Wiley & Sons.

6

God is Change: Beyond Creation Care

Persephone

Persephone is my deadline. After this point in early November, there is no longer the day length required for plants to grow. They will resume their growth at the inverse and opposite point next spring. Persephone is the goddess of spring, abducted into underworlds. The abduction can feel sudden, if anticipated. There is a certain loss and some anxiety when the growth we've come to love goes away. Are we prepared to survive this winter? Now is the time we live with the consequences; we cannot pause this deepening. We cannot go back without first descending, then climbing back up and through.

As the seasons irreversibly change, we reflect on where we've been and where we are going. We discern the impacts of our action and its limits. We face the facts and come to terms both with what we have done and what we have left undone. The season's change is thrust upon us, like the climate change with which we all must now live, regardless of contributions or culpabilities past.

Each change induces anxieties of its own. While one change is natural, inevitable and even welcome, the change in patterns of change is looming and chaotic. Where, in winter, the sudden loss of productivity is a welcome relief and respite, proven to feed a new season's growth and renew its cycle, the decline that accompanies climate breakdown is more a devolution, and its outcomes are more uncertain. The deepening darkness of winter anticipates light's return. Perhaps the same is true of this.

We all must live with the consequences of the carbon already unleashed from its underworld, threatening us with the terrifying power some gave it readily. We pray those who did this will be held to account. Heated homes through winter compound the summer's extreme heat at this orbit's opposite end. Persephone reemerges unpredictably now: in buds on fruit trees too soon before the threat of frost has passed, or in blooms out of sync with their pollinating companions.

The change we made is the change we fear. While change has forever been constant, today's change is erratic and threatening. How do we prepare for this winter, this change so far from predictable? The only instructions that feel stable are those that invite me to abandon the desire for fixity:

> *All that you touch, you change*
>   *All that you change, changes you*
>   *The only lasting truth is change*
>   *God is change.*[1]

Feedback loops

Climate change is a contraction, making once-habitable environments unsuitable for human futures and causing global migrations that will rework and reshape planetary footprints, shrinking the places future humans may live.[2] Climate change means vanishing coastlines, once-fertile alluvial beds made desert or returning to water, whole desert regions becoming, if not yet parched, unbearably hot.

As threats magnify and precipitate, we feed the agents of still more change: air conditioning causes heat islands in need of more cooling, water diverted from farmland to development puts those homes in harm's way where surrounding land is dry and water scarce. Today's adaptations can make future adaptation more difficult. On the coldest days, fragile grids are overrun. Our life support systems seem prone to failure at the very moments we need their regulation most. We seek to ameliorate the worst impacts of fossil fuel-driven change with solutions that deepen the crisis.[3] Technologies that interrupt constant change, as refrigeration interrupts spoilage,[4] may cause us to temporarily forget the earth's constant change. But their subduction of the earth is temporary and incomplete, magnifying disturbances elsewhere in the system, testifying to the fundamental aliveness of the earth.

Our lives in this modern world create positive feedback loops. Though we live in a world transformed, the earth is still alive, responsive to disturbance and increasingly unruly. Our efforts to resist change come back to us as change of a different kind. As we continue down the road we've called progress, our collective habit trails further erode the path. The paths we walk are the paths we ordain, and though this ordination is an accident of aggregated choice, the way we go is the way we make easier for those who come next.

The food and energy systems that sustain our lives have their own metabolism. The city and the country exist in relation, each made possible by the exchange of energy and capital between them.[5] These corridors are made visible only when working improperly, or when carrying threats like infectious disease. Exporting food and water to faraway marketplaces can obscure this essential fact, causing demand to balloon where the costs of consumption are externalized and invisible. As supply chains grow and become more complex and opaque, they are more vulnerable to disruption. So, too, land heavily managed and controlled can respond to its confinement abruptly: conserved land stokes urban firestorms; floodwaters funnelled through concrete corridors drown. Though heavily managed and transformed, matter – *land* – continues to reveal itself as vital, brimming, moving, lively and ever-changing, despite our best attempts to control its course.[6]

There is seasonal change with which farmers are familiar. We change with a changing earth that propels our movement – through seasons and axial tilts – changing our behaviour and our task list constantly as it moves. In winter, darkening hours usher us inside for intimate gatherings, sharing the heat of our bodies between longer hours of sleep. As days brighten and lengthen, as we are propelled outward towards the sun which comes closer, we harness a seasonal peak in solar energy alongside the fruiting plants that do the same. Inside our bodies, there are smaller cycles: diurnal cycles of stimulation and rest, and cycles that mimic moon phases.

Climate change is change on another scale. This change is less cyclical and more destabilizing – a change to the patterns of constant change we've built our societies and cultures to accommodate. The break is felt when winter rituals arrive with haunting heat. This is not predictable like seasons. As the ground shifts under our feet in fissures and landslides, subsidence pulls land into depths pumped dry but not recharged. The seasons whose changes we've come to expect are themselves changing: the eerie enjoyment of warm winters disregulates our minds and bodies.

This change in the patterns of change emerges and intensifies as a failure of adaptation. Climate change is complex and has multiple anthropogenic causes, but a primary cause of its intractability is the resistance to the change as refusal to adapt. The irony is that, in resisting the change that is required of us, we cause destabilizing change to intensify.[7] We change the planetary through the force of a world *not* changing in response to the warnings that climate scientists have been sounding for decades.[8]

There is comfort in the denial of climate change, just as there is in the idea of an unchanging god. The pain of inevitable loss – whether personal or planetary – may be ameliorated by assurances of eternal life or an eternal god. So many people of faith accept climate change as the world's foretold falling away and damnation, while resisting change in response to a human-changed climate. *The earth changes and God stays the same* – but what if we have this all wrong?

The consequences of anthropogenic climate change unleash compounding disasters. We might call them acts of God, except they are our own. Not ours individually or evenly, but in aggregate and driven most by the wealthiest. The human is both you and me, and *us* collectively. The scale of our actions is comprehensible at an individual level, but we struggle to comprehend the scale of our collective action. It is in this way that we humans – individuals with varying degrees of power – act as the mythic 'human', as God acts upon the world. The pronouncement 'you are gods' is becoming more true each day as humans cause changes in the weather.

Humans unleash a change we must now navigate, though no one can control the change humans are unleashing. The human is nearly omnipotent in destructive capacity, and yet our individual and shared powers to ameliorate this destruction are partial. 'The human' acts in aggregate, and yet you and I function as mere mortals. The human of the Anthropocene is mythic; those of us who constitute that human have limited agency – diluted as it is distributed – to control or direct such godlike power – so long as we act alone.

No longer are we powerless in the face of an omnipotent god. No longer does God alone control the weather, or determine the limits of the sea's proud waves.[9] The power with which we must reckon looks different, unwieldy, as it is distributed across many agents, deeper timescales and wider geographies. The power of the human-become-god has caused contractions both spatial and temporal. The carbon we unleash constitutes a kind of time travel – as we release the embodied energy of ancient, buried ones, sacrifice land to sea-level rise, and bring the end of time ever closer.

Transforming climate anxiety

When we contemplate what's coming, we do so with dread, unable to imagine, between the headlines and the models, a future better for our youngers than this one is for us. Facing a future of a *more* changed climate, hardwired trauma-responses make us fight, freeze and run.[10] We feel guilt for what we do, but we flee from these feelings in apathy, convincing ourselves that what we do does not matter. Nihilistically, we diminish the significance of the great losses we face, or we dread them so much we are paralysed. We are outraged at the perpetrators of lies and profiteering – and too often at their victims, too. We fight to protect a revisionist history already irrecoverable; or, in wilful ignorance, we turn from the truth and turn inward, to self-care or enjoyment of the time we have left, shrinking our spheres of concern.

As we wait for this bleak future, some will attempt to encourage, diminishing the significance of this tense present by alluding to a past that was harder, or worse, or the same. Whether the anxieties, injustices and uncertainties are similar or different now doesn't matter much, as the devastation, dread and doom we face are clearly unsettling us collectively. The hope and optimism that old progress narratives impose are old seeds with declining germination rates. We can't believe these tired stories anymore because we have considered all the facts. Those with a future to anticipate do not know how to anticipate the future – knowing too much of the problem but knowing too little what to do. Those who would guide them do not know what is coming any better than young people do. The survival tactics the seasoned have learned and the rules for success they proffer may well become obsolete in a world dramatically changed, a world that cannot bear more growth of this kind.

Our actions propel change. We live with the awareness that we are changing the ecosystems upon which we depend with every move. But our actions must also respond to the changes we are making. The god of Octavia Butler's *Parable of the Sower* is not worshipped but shaped, is not stability, but change.[11] The god of change stands in defiance of an unchanging, eternal god. Those who follow this god learn to work with the chaotic change of a climate-changed world.

The alternative is cognitive dissonance: the discomfort we feel when our actions and perceived identity are out of step. If climate change is made worse by our resistance to it, cognitive dissonance worsens our situation by keeping us from facing the change we create. Self-justification ameliorates cognitive dissonance temporarily as a self-preservative strategy, steeling us against what threatens to break us down.[12] But anxiety still comes to a head in daily decisions where consequences are difficult to comprehend. Martin Luther is said to have promoted planting apple trees, even at the end of the world.

To plant an apple tree today is a question of futurity and ethics. These garden beds are made of materials that are themselves ruins of the industrial age: railroad ties caked in creosote, carbonaceous chemicals derived from tar and coal used to preserve tracks laid by immigrants from rot, repurposed by those who stayed here through older boom and bust cycles. Now, those chemicals, leached from sun-bleached wood, make their way into the bodies of plants and their pollinators and into my own as well. I debate planting edible plants in these beds, an effort to protect myself from known risks. Then I consider that every plant is someone's food. The nearly domesticated deer have found safer harbour in our neighbourhoods than in the woods where predators and chronic wasting disease pose threats. Would planting perennials for pollinators in contaminated soils cause these contaminants to be taken up by the insects and birds I wish to feed? To plant is to demonstrate some measure of hope, to make possible futures. But the futures that feel possible from this vantage are compromised, carrying forward the sins of the past.

Climate chaos, catastrophe, collapse all signal contracting possibilities. The work of the farmer is to make possible futures. But these futures are hard to imagine today, when so much of what we see forecloses possibility. Forever chemical contamination is now ubiquitous in land and water, and it is this land and this water that feed and nourish us and our children, living and unborn. Our children come from this soil. We will return our children to this soil. Our children will come from this soil again.

How do we go on in compromised environments – where soil is contaminated and microplastics already move everywhere, not only through hydrological cycles and soil profiles but through our epidermal and cellular walls? There is nowhere untouched by the fallout of industrial capitalism and nowhere to hide from its consequences. That the soils from which we eat are marked by the violence of war: from the Haber–Bosch process that adapted the tool of chemical warfare to accelerate production, to the aerial attacks – Agent Orange, glyphosate, white phosphorus – that sought to stymie the food production of those deemed adversaries in Vietnam, Colombia,[13] and Palestine, that Holy, promised Land terrorized and decimated by the bombs of the chosen.

Climate anxiety, at its root, fears the loss and disintegration of those worlds and those selves we have protected and known, even knowing what harm our fictions cause our places and our spirits. The anxiety persists when we insist on the preservation of economic dogmas based ineluctably on the extraction of value and vitality from places we cannot really see nor understand. We insist on the idea of our own holy sanctification, separate from while still inside a world condemned, as if we, our bodies and our cognition, were not made of the same, humming, cosmic matter our acts disparage. Climate anxiety is the cognitive dissonance of knowing what we do hurts us, for we are of and with the earth. Climate anxiety fears the loss of self-stable worlds, yet knows these have always been a fiction. Climate anxiety grieves change it does not anticipate, and yet accelerates, as it threatens the constitution of a self that is passing away.

Towards experience

Students entrapped in cycles of anxiety and white Christians inheriting a Protestant work ethic like to ask the question 'What do I do?' as a way of ameliorating guilt. It is a lifelong question, one we should always be asking. But what we should do changes moment to moment, season to season, and depends on the needs and concerns of our neighbours and the places we make. What we can do in the meantime is pay attention.

I learn the art of attention from farmers, who cannot survive or navigate the constant change of caring for a field without it. Every season marks a change but, year to year, seasons change differently: bringing insect, economic or weed pressures surely different from those of the year before. Year to year, countless variables contribute to the outcomes with which we contend, whose ultimate sources are always an educated guess. The work of the farmer is relentlessly involved: there is no way to track all that is going on. But a good and seasoned farmer pays attention to an environment of constant change, all its variability and minutiae, and weathers whatever storm it brings, knowing it will pass. A farmer notes changes that happen in patterns, and also when patterns shift. The land enfolds patterns, but does not work like a machine. It is never wholly legible to its 'users'. The lexicons and tools we use to model and foretell its behaviour are never complex enough. Backyard soil science can describe the soil's texture and type, even read its history in its striation standing in a soil pit, or identify the macro and micronutrients in abundance or deficit for plant performance, but there is so much, too, that these ways of knowing cannot do.

It takes experience, repeated, holding soil in the hand. Not just any soil but the soil of the place where you are, and not just any hand but yours, to know when it is time to work. And this knowledge is based on relative weight, density and soil saturation, paying attention to the temperature and the forecast and the rate of evaporation, and how this soil pedon breaks apart into aggregates in your hand or on the ground, compared to yesterday. It takes experience to anticipate when your plant companions will wilt under pressure and to foretell the season's change and the cabbage moths' lifecycle well enough to have what you need at that time. It takes experience of that too-early sweat in the rush of summer to prepare oneself again for it in the frozen standstill of winter – this physical memory of seasonal change – and to adapt oneself to it, to mark time by it, to live with and not against it.

In the Protestant tradition I inherited, experience is one of the primary ways we seek to know an unknowable God. Scripture, tradition, reason and *experience* all inform one another equally. Martín Prechtel advises learning as much as we can firsthand as a rule for living.[14] A famer does this, knowing there is no substitute for experience with the land.

It strikes me that my frustrations and discomforts with farming have much more to do with my inexperience than with the land itself. I asked an older farmer once, digging through beds of carrots by hand, whether she ever got mad at the land. She looked at me with a piercing inquisitiveness, and after a long pause said very calmly that the experience of frustration is more likely and more often a problem with the person, rather than a problem with the land that is the object of one's anger. I'm not sure if she was relating to my feeling or calling me to account, but in any case it caused me to look deeper and to ask why exactly I was finding myself so frequently arrived at anger. A puzzling emotion to feel in such a bucolic setting. How was it that such an intense emotion festered so long to the point of eruption? I was angry with the land for not cooperating with my expectations, for not meeting my ideals for what it should be already or should yet become, for asking what I thought was too much. It comes from being out of sync, not attuned to rhythms you cannot control but can only learn. It comes from being novice enough to consistently ask too much of the land under your care, or not enough of yourself or your co-labourers, or to be so shortsighted as to underestimate the work to come, seasonal shifts and their accompanying threats, or to misunderstand life's eternal dance with death.

Another friend, in mid-July, when the farmer's life is hardest, advised I adopt a mindfulness practice of 'farm Zen'. In July, it's too late to change the course of unfolding chaos. Farm Zen is a choice to engage only selectively in reparative work, when the time is right and your power is useful, but detaching from desired outcomes when efforts are futile to change the way things are headed.[15] We were speaking of cucumbers, diseased by the tiny toothmarks of ten thousand beetles, and whether to apply the powdery pesticide or whether it was already too late. Do you kill them, or let them live, let them take the cucumbers you would struggle to save anyway, and plant another succession next year? Next time, we will anticipate their reemergence and adjust our preventative maintenance plans and expectations accordingly.

It is a stoic principle to apportion one's care selectively to those things within one's control and to limit one's care for those that lie outside it. This honest analysis is useful to the farmer day to day, but also unrealistic in a world where the highest matters of concern seem entirely out of our control. Do we forego care for that which seems impossible to change? Do we forge different kinds of care? Or is it a different sense of agency we need, a bigger and broader definition of what is within our control at a moment when we act more collectively than individually upon our environments – atmospherically? Who and how would 'we' need to be to make the changes necessary for our survival?

Experience modifies our behaviour, ambitions and expectations, and also shows us how small we are alone and where our efforts amplify one another. Experience is embodied knowledge that allows us to adapt to new ways of life and anticipate its constant change. The knowledge we gain through experience in so many seasonal attempts to shape the land and its behaviour always ends up shaping us back, and more.

From creation care, towards caring, creating

A growing movement among the religious concerns itself with 'creation care', where care for the creation is conceived as the duty of the faithful. But what is it that we name 'creation'? What does this category exclude? Are humans part of the creation, or is creation that untouched wilderness that is so much a human creation,[16] separating the human and more-than-human worlds? The creation we speak of is *broad*, containing all that we profess God has made: everything that crawls upon the earth and inside us, the beasts of the sea, the plants, the planets. Creation is nearly inconceivable. Flattening more life and landforms than we can imagine into a single, two-dimensional word can easily become a substitute for awareness.

For me, growing up, creation was peaks summited at sunrise or the view from the ridge, a big, fiery sky marking each day's end, the bull moose munching willows a few inches from my tent, the howling wind or lightning storms that made me afraid for my life. This creation is dramatic and loud, and it seeks attention: where the weather and the climate converse as snowpack, drought conditions and fire danger. Where geological history and cooled lava flows determine our path, and where our orientation is always anchored by mountains to the west. Where southern exposure makes for good climbing on a cold day but also avalanches in winter and rattlesnakes in summer. The land is felt in its connectivity; we see from high vistas how glaciers formed valleys and plains. It was wilderness, 'untrammelled',[17] distanced from traces left by human hands. The city upon this creation was understood as a clear imposition.

From inside the city, creation appears as an aberration, imprisoned in parcels, reserves amid seas of development struggling to land somewhere or come up for air. Creation here is subdued to quiet manageability or reworked towards profit's potential, silenced so as to naturalize the ongoing colonial moves to which it is subjected as property. When we speak of the creation, of what do we speak? Of the untrammelled, itself a construction, or that which is evidently managed? In either case, the creation is an idea whose 'care' is nowhere near straightforward, because creation is not static – it does not function like a bank account, where good deeds are credited and bad deeds are debited against a diminishing resource pool. Creation – unlike the 'resources' into which we transform it – is alive and inherently regenerative. It is responsive to feedbacks, often in unpredictable ways, as it may transform our benevolent acts into unintended consequences or redeem our malevolent ones. In an age of climate breakdown, what we have called creation is speaking louder to us. The land – its waters – rises up now, to speak something about who and what and where we are and what this land desires to be.

Care for creation is not merely feeling, but skill, study, training, receptivity and attentiveness. Care is not abstract, but what we practise, a habituated relation to an alive creation. Care – neither universal nor abstract – implies obligation and cultivates responsibility.

While so many world-ending crises compete for our attention, we say we cannot afford to care. We place limits on our empathy so that we may survive the cruelty. This form of care is limited by our cognitive capacity, a non-renewable resource – conceptual and abstract – that comes down to feeling and tends towards discouragement. This care produces overwhelm, as we are overwhelmed by the manifold tragedies for which we *ought* to care but are prevented by our self-protective capacities of cognitive dissonance, *and* by our felt impotence to enact the repair that feels necessary. But those who *practise* care know that care is a muscle whose exercise builds strength. Expanding the breadth and depth of our care may feel terrifying, but its practice deepens the well from which to draw, as it strengthens relations with the object of care, and receives care, devotion and attention reciprocally from a living creation.

I wonder whether our care is wide enough for the not-so-charismatic, deep enough to include care for the inanimate and inorganic that also create living worlds – for the toxins and pollutants proliferating in soils and waters. Care that these externalities signal something, care to know what they want to say. This is the care of attentiveness, and it is not foreclosed: care as curiosity, care as inquiry, care as prayer. Care as staking one's matters of concern in the ground somewhere, a ground one seeks to know. Only then, with the expectation of accountability in place, made by patient and practised and just relation, does the question of what to do and how to enact one's care become possible.

'Creation care' may inadvertently imply that those doing the caring and the object of that care were separable in the first place, creating an inequality of importance in which humans dole out their scarce care to so-called human concerns, while forgetting that they too are creation. As if these human stewards saw and judged creation from above, the way we might imagine a deistic god to do: moving chips, striking lightning, commanding and executing at will, bestowing or withholding gifts. But creation is not 'out there', not something we can touch or observe from a distance. Creation is the conditions that make our observation possible. Creation is not just what we see but the *way* we see. Creation is *how* we care. We are the creation.

So when creation is changing, it is also asking us to change. Soon the request will not be a choice – if we do not move, we will be moved,[18] if not by disaster then by its consequences, urging us toward new practices of care and new language.[19]

With words, we make and unmake worlds. Our words are acts of creation: consecrating or condemning. *In the beginning was the word.* Our praise protects, our directives destroy. Priestly language – prayer and policy – forms, re-forms, de-forms creation. We make places through permissions and prohibitions that consecrate and desecrate. State-sanctioned sacrifices to economic growth hollow our mountains and fill dumps, while rocks called cathedrals we touch only carefully.

God is a gardener

In the beginning, God hovered over waters; since land's emergence, God has touched the ground. We make God in the image of aspirations: of ease and leisure, distanced from dirt. Mortals desiring knowledge and power work tirelessly to remake themselves in the image of this imagined god, omniscient and omnipotent. But God is a gardener, trading omnipotence for immanence, the eternal for impermanence, in becoming human of humus.

While God was in the garden, humans have become gods, immortal through radioactivity and Styrofoam, omniscient through surveillance capitalism,[20] omnipotent in the weird and deadly weather unleashed in an atmosphere changed by human hands. Our tractors run on big data, tethered to the cloud, which is after all not in the sky but in warehouses of thirsty servers in deserts out of sight. These tools transform the land they touch into numeric representations of reality that cannot speak back. They destroy the heavenly paradise for which they long, sacrificing it on a table to feed this world that continues to cannibalize the next.

The expertise of a gardener is made with dirt under the nails, a test of love's commitment. It is involved, and it is not indifferent. Just as the space and time are affected by ever-changing rain patterns, sunlight hours and seasons, the grower, too, is squishy, porous, changeable. It is not – was never – about being in control, but about being in the rhythms and seasons you know you can't control. Gardening is always an act of faith, with outcomes never ordained or guaranteed.

Where was God in the garden? They knew God directly then. Only after the fall did the work of feeding oneself become toil. Is this the birth of agriculture?[21] The inauguration of a certain gendered division of labour: Eve's reproductive and gestative, Adam's productive and earthy? Some name pain, others labour as the fate to which we are exiled. Except the first humans did work in the garden, too. So what was Adam's curse?

Perhaps the curse was already evident in the act itself – not the loss of omniscience, but the desire for it. Perhaps we live now with the fallout of this arrogance. When we have become god, there is no other god to save us. It is ours alone to decide how we will change with climate change. Perhaps we could give up our entitlements, join in the work and pay attention. Not with the expectation of some grand eschaton, but to release what makes us desire the ultimacy of extinction over the uncertainty of adaptation. Season after season, we tend again and again the change that is coming for us already, from the almighty. Joining God in the garden, perhaps we can learn to survive.

Seeds: a prayer

The more I dig, the more I uncover seeds in me. They find water, light and air and they germinate. I wait to see what takes root. So many dormant seeds in the soil, some nourishing, others competitive and destructive. Where did these seeds come from? What plants will these seeds make? What memories do they carry, touched by different places and different hands? They continue to live only by finding root in this soil. They will adapt to this place over time, and I will, with them, do the same.

God is change. Which god do we work with? The god resisting change while causing more, or the God who works in the garden, changing with it, season after season?

Notes

1 Octavia E. Butler, 2000, *The Parable of the Sower*, reprint edn, Grand Central Publishing, p. 3 (first published 1993).

2 Bill McKibben, 2019, *Falter: Has the Human Game Begun to Play Itself Out?*, Henry Holt and Company.

3 Wendell Berry, 2003, 'Solving for Pattern', in Norman Wirzba (ed.), *The Art of the Commonplace: The Agrarian Essays of Wendell Berry*, Counterpoint, pp. 267–78.

4 Nicola Twilley, 2024, *Frostbite: How Refrigeration Changed Our Food, Our Planet, and Ourselves*, Penguin.

5 John Bellamy Foster, 'Marx's Theory of Metabolic Rift: Classical Foundations for Environmental Sociology', *American Journal of Sociology*, 105(2) (1999), pp. 366–405, https://doi.org/10.1086/210315.

6 Jane Bennett, 2010, *Vibrant Matter: A Political Ecology of Things*, Duke University Press.

7 Naomi Klein, 2015, *This Changes Everything: Capitalism vs. the Climate*, Simon and Schuster.

8 J. Hansen et al., 'Climate Impact of Increasing Atmospheric Carbon Dioxide', *Science*, 213(4511) (1981), pp. 957–66, https://doi.org/10.1126/science.213.4511.957.

9 Job 38.8.

10 Leslie Davenport, 2017, 'The Psychology of Climate Change Denial', in *Emotional Resiliency in the Era of Climate Change: A Clinician's Guide*, Jessica Kingsley Publishers, pp. 35–40.

11 Butler, *The Parable of the Sower*.

12 Carol Tavris, 2013, *Mistakes Were Made (but Not by Me): Why We Justify Foolish Beliefs, Bad Decisions and Hurtful Acts*, Pinter & Martin Limited.

13 Kristina M. Lyons, 2020, *Vital Decomposition: Soil Practitioners and Life Politics*, Duke University Press.

14 Martín Prechtel, 2015, *The Smell of Rain on Dust: Grief and Praise*, North Atlantic Books, p. 157.

15 This idea comes from my friend Gabe, who helped me learn how to farm.

16 William Cronon, 'The Trouble with Wilderness: Or, Getting Back to the Wrong Nature', *Environmental History*, 1(1) (1996), pp. 7–28, https://doi.org/10.2307/3985059.

17 Wilderness Act of 1964 (USA).

18 Tyson Yunkaporta, 2020, *Sand Talk: How Indigenous Thinking Can Save the World*, HarperCollins.

19 Amitav Ghosh, 2022, *The Nutmeg's Curse: Parables for a Planet in Crisis*, University of Chicago Press.

20 Shoshana Zuboff, 2019, *The Age of Surveillance Capitalism: The Fight for a Human Future at the New Frontier of Power*, PublicAffairs. See also Hanna Reichel, 2019, 'Worldmaking Knowledge: What the Doctrine of Omniscience Can Help Us Understand about Digitization (Part I)', *Cursor_Zeitschrift für explorative Theologie*, https://doi.org/10.21428/fb61f6aa.34c88e75.

21 S. Lily Mendoza, 2018, 'Composting Civilization's Grief: Life, Love, and Learning in a Time of Eco-Apocalypse', in Eileen R. Tabios (ed.), *Humanity: An Anthology, Volume 1*, Paloma Press, pp. 118–36.

www.ingramcontent.com/pod-product-compliance
Lightning Source LLC
Chambersburg PA
CBHW022017290426
44109CB00015B/1207